Jimmy
and Me

Joyce Poggi-Hager

Also by JOYCE POGGI HAGER

Musing Off the Mat

Jimmy
and Me

A SISTER'S MEMOIR

JOYCE POGGI HAGER

Some names and identifying characteristics in this book have
been changed to protect the privacy of individuals.

ISBN-10: 1530596955
ISBN-13: 978-1530596959

Library of Congress Control Number: 2017912087

CreateSpace Independent Publishing Platform
North Charleston, SC

For Kristin and Melissa

If a man does not keep pace with his companions,
perhaps it is because he hears a different drummer.
Let him step to the music which he hears,
however measured or far away.

- Henry David Thoreau

1

When I saw the caller ID that Sunday night, my heart raced. It always does when the social worker calls. It means there's a problem with my brother.

"We're waiting for the psychological team to come and assess Jimmy. He said he was going to jump off the balcony tonight."

My throat tightened. *Oh my God. Now what do I do?*

This wasn't the first time Jimmy said he wanted to kill himself. He'd been depressed and agitated since our mother died four years earlier. This time, though, he didn't only say he wanted to die. This time he had specified a plan.

"It could be a few hours until the team arrives to evaluate Jimmy and make a recommendation," said the social worker. "We'll stay with him."

"What should I do?"

"Sit tight. I'll call you when I have more information."

I debated whether to try sleeping or pack my bags and get in the car. I'd driven to Jimmy's apartment several times before to resolve crises but nothing like this. If I stayed home, I'd feel guilty. If I went, I wasn't guaranteed to be with Jimmy or even be helpful. Scared that fatigue and exhaustion would overwhelm me on the five-hour drive in the dark, I decided to wait for the call then determine what to do next.

I spent a sleepless, windy November night pacing the floor of my home in Massachusetts, more than 300 miles away. My heart ached for Jimmy in New Jersey. He had people supporting him but no family nearby. Surely he must be feeling alone, too.

The next day, my birthday, was worse. I walked around the house in a state of despair and isolation. My daughters were away at college and my husband had pressure at work. I couldn't tell my two sisters what was happening. They were in Pennsylvania taking care of our 85-year-old father. Hurricane Sandy had forced Dad from his home one week earlier. We were unsure if his house was still standing.

I padded from room to room on tenterhooks, yanking my hair, waiting for the phone to ring with any news. Was I being a neglectful sister for not jumping in the car and forcing myself past the medical professionals? Would my love be enough medication or did he need more than I could provide?

How did the boy with the hearty laugh who used to walk to school with me become a man desperate enough to want to end his life? I couldn't imagine what my brother was going through alone in his bedroom with staff watching his every move. Would they pack clean clothes for him? Were they holding his hand? I wanted to talk to him, comfort him, put my arms around him, tell him everything would be okay. I wanted to tell him how much I loved him and that he had much to live for.

Later I learned they had taken him from his supervised apartment to the local emergency room where he stayed for thirty-six hours before being transferred to a state psychiatric hospital. There he had been stripped of all his belongings. He wasn't allowed to read a newspaper, something he loved to do. Jimmy had only known a warm, comfortable home his whole life and had the freedom to come and go as he pleased. Now he was confined with the bare essentials in a cold, small, cinder block room with a bed bolted to the floor. I imagined his room was more like a jail cell than a place to recover. He'd have to use an electric shaver for the first time in his life. He wouldn't feel sunlight for seven days.

Once again, I saw my life repeating itself as his advocate and keeper. Would I have the strength to help Jimmy this time? There was no choice. I knew my role. I had to get him out. I had to work with the doctors and nurses and social workers and get him back. Back to the Jimmy I knew before he became emotionally absent and started taking meds that clearly were not working.

2

The first time my older brother Jimmy was placed in my mother's arms, she sensed something wrong. The obstetrician assured her that the baby was healthy and the delivery uneventful. At home, Jimmy was a docile baby, but Mom's instincts gnawed at her. When she expressed concerns about Jimmy's hearing, and later, difficulty crawling, the pediatrician answered, "Boys are slower to develop," suggesting Mom shouldn't compare Jimmy to his older sister. When Mom reported that Jimmy had failed to talk by the age of two, the doctor responded, "Give him time." Each time Mom reported another missed developmental milestone, the doctor dismissed her as an anxious mother and said, "Wait."

By the time I was five, I knew Jimmy was different but didn't know how or why. He wasn't like my two sisters or me, or any of the other kids on the block. Jimmy didn't talk much. When he did, he often mumbled. He wore tortoise-shell glasses. He used his left hand instead of his right like everyone else in our family. He never tucked his shirt in all the way and the buttons were usually off by one. He walked like a duck and tripped a lot. When my mother talked on the phone, I often heard her say the words "mentally retarded."

"What does mentally retarded mean?" I asked several times.

"To retard means to slow," she'd answer quite seriously. "Jimmy is slow." And that was the end of the conversation.

My mother read a lot. When I asked Mom how she knew something, she usually answered, "I read it somewhere." She kept two oversized dictionaries with dark red covers on the shelf of her nightstand. One was a regular dictionary and the other read Medical Dictionary on the spine. I could tell Mom used the medical dictionary more than the other one because its pages had separated from the spine, tiny white threads hanging from the top and bottom of its cover.

Mom would lick her right pointer finger and turn the tissue-thin pages from the top corner. Her brown eyes scanned the pages up and down, back and forth. Then she'd put the fingers of her left hand between pages to save a spot. Those books were the only things on her shelf, besides a box of tissues. Sometimes in the morning crumpled tissues lay on the floor by her side of the bed. I'd see more tissues over the years, on Dad's side of the bed, too.

As a kid, I knew slow meant the opposite of fast, but Mom's explanation didn't make sense to me. Slow doing what? I'd seen Jimmy run. He didn't run fast but he didn't run slowly either. He walked up and down the stairs differently from the rest of the family. Instead of putting one foot on a step and the other foot on the next step, he'd put one foot and then the other foot on each step, before going to the next.

"Goy-kee," he'd say, trailing me in the house. That's what Jimmy used to call me: Goy-kee. He couldn't pronounce the "J" in Joyce, and he gave me the extra -kee for Joycie. He'd breathe open-mouthed and often drool from his plump lower lip. He wore thick glasses after having had several surgeries to tighten the muscles behind his eyes.

In order to take Jimmy to doctor appointments all over Philadelphia, Dad taught Mom how to drive in her early twenties. She'd pile all four kids, unbuckled, into the massive blue and white 1955 Chevrolet Bel Air. Lynne, the first, was four years older than me. Alison, the baby, was four years younger. Jimmy and I sandwiched in between. We'd crank the windows down and peer out from the back seat at neighborhoods that looked different than ours. Those houses were situated close together with hardly any trees or grass in tiny yards. Yellow taxicabs swarmed the roads.

"Lock the doors," Mom would tell us.

On one drive into Philadelphia, Mom got lost in an unsafe section of the city.

"Now which way should I turn?" she said half to herself. In the rearview mirror, she noticed Jimmy pointing left. Jimmy always had a fantastic memory. When the game show *Concentration* came on TV, he'd beat us all. Mom took a leap of faith and decided to turn left. When we reached the doctor's office, Mom exhaled, turned to Jimmy and said, "Jimmy, you knew the way, didn't you? What would I do without you?"

Although Jimmy's diagnosis was mental retardation, my parents still wanted to know how his brain cells became damaged. So she drove to appointment after appointment, but the medical professionals couldn't offer an explanation.

"Put him away. He'll never amount to anything," said more than one doctor.

My mother refused. She persisted in her quest for answers and care for Jimmy. She booked yet another appointment with Dr. Spitz, the famous pediatric neurosurgeon at Children's Hospital of Philadelphia. Somehow, she managed to jump ahead of dozens of patients from all over the world waiting to see him. Dr. Spitz gave my parents hope. He recommended a new treatment called "patterning."

Patterning was an innovative type of physical therapy in the early 1960s recommended for people with mental retardation and brain injury. It simulated crawling. Its goal was to increase oxygen flow to the brain. Dr. Spitz convinced Mom and Dad that patterning, combined with other breathing and physical exercises, might help Jimmy achieve improved to "normal" development with everyday tasks, motor coordination, and even intellect.

The basement was the only space in our modest, three-bedroom home where we could pattern Jimmy. Dad built a sturdy table to support his only son. We began patterning Jimmy when he was six. The table was a simple 4x8 piece of plywood nailed onto a couple of wooden sawhorses. My father covered the plywood with padding and stapled a plastic tablecloth over it so Jimmy could move more easily. Together, we moved all the

We lived on the right side of this twin home on Stoneybrook Lane
where we patterned Jimmy in the basement.
Drexel Hill, Pennsylvania

15

tools, boots, toys, containers, and junk out of the way to make room for the new patterning table.

Our whole neighborhood got involved. Super-organized Aunt Anna wrote up a schedule after recruiting neighbors to volunteer for the patterning shifts. Annie (as she was called by Mom) was my mother's best friend who lived down the street and visited often. Although not my real aunt, I'd always known her as Aunt Anna and loved the sound of her name rolling off my tongue.

"Rosemarie!" she'd call out for my mother in a singsong voice as she breezed in carrying a brown lunch bag full of Philadelphia soft pretzels for us. Aunt Anna was a petite woman. You couldn't help noticing her when she entered a room. She always stood up straight, wore make-up smelling like a fresh-cut bouquet of flowers, and wore clothes looking like she had just ironed them. She'd drink coffee and smoke cigarettes with Mom. Her laugh reminded me of the giggles from the lady munchkins in the Land of Oz.

The DiCanzio, DiGiorgio, Carfagno, Moretto, Marturano, and Verdi families were a demonstrative and loving group. Their smiles lit up the room when they walked in the front door. I liked our house being the center of attention with all the neighbors chatting and laughing in the living room.

"It's time to pattern Jimmy," said Mom one morning, tucking a loose strand of red hair back into her French twist. "We only have four volunteers today, Joyce, so you have to be the fifth and take the lead this time."

I gazed up at her with my mouth wide open from the living room floor where a doll rested in my arms. What could she have been thinking? I was only five years old, one year younger than Jimmy. I'd been watching the adults do it for months but never got assigned one of Jimmy's body parts. My entire body tightened.

"I'll be back soon," I whispered to my doll as I laid her in a canopy bed for a nap.

I led the neighbors down the narrow, creaky stairs to our basement and watched as they squished around the table to take their places. The single bulb hanging from the center of the ceiling cast a dull green hue in the dreary room. In a narrow hallway leading to the back door, our washer and dryer banged and whirred. A glint of sunlight filtered in.

It felt weird to be at the head of the table because usually I sat on the stairs and watched. I didn't know if I could hold and turn Jimmy's head with my hands for five minutes. I worried about breaking the rhythm and yearned to be upstairs with Mom and my baby sister Alison.

Slowly and silently, Jimmy climbed onto the patterning table in his cotton pajamas, belly side down. Sometimes he'd mumble or moan—likely to self-soothe—but he always did as he was told and never complained. Jimmy often squirmed on the table until the adults put their hands on him to help settle him down.

In my nightgown, I timidly stepped onto a stool to reach Jimmy. Someone set the white kitchen timer for five minutes. There wasn't any time for me to think about it because everyone turned to me, waiting for a signal. I assumed my role, as Mom had told me, and led the group. I held my older brother's head with his damaged brain in the palms of my hands. This bellwether physical act would lead to a lifetime of responsibility.

The quintet helped Jimmy simulate crawling as his body lay flat against the table. While Mrs. Verdi held Jimmy's knee and ankle to bend his right leg, Aunt Anna held Jimmy's elbow and wrist to move his right arm forward, palm down by his nose.

The neighbors chatted during the session and soon Mrs. Verdi and Mrs. DiGiorgio laughed about something.

"Theresa, keep up!" Aunt Anna said.

"I'm trying, Annie," replied Mrs. Verdi. "His leg is heavy, you know. You have it easier moving his arm."

"Don't break the rhythm," Aunt Anna directed.

On the other side of the table, Mrs. DiGiorgio straightened Jimmy's left leg while Mrs. Carfagno moved Jimmy's left arm back, palm side up, on top of his butt. I moved Jimmy's head side to side, keeping the rhythm.

"How much more time, Annie?" Mrs. DiGiorgio asked.

"Another minute," replied Aunt Anna, squinting at the timer.

Back and forth. Back and forth. This way. That way. Flip. Flap. Flip. Flap. Even though I led the group, I felt alone in the midst of the adult conversation. Jimmy must have felt alone, too. We patterned alone, together.

Halfway through the patterning set I saw Jimmy drooling, leaving a wet spot on the tablecloth. I thought that tiny puddle must have annoyed him, rubbing against his cheeks. I wanted to wipe it clean but couldn't break the rhythm. I remember repeating a pattern to myself: How . . . long . . . do I . . . have to . . . do this? My arms ached. With each turn, a muffled thump and swish sounded on the padded cover of the table. Flip. Flap. Flip. Flap.

Beads of sweat trickled along Jimmy's hairline as he lifted his head. Usually he closed his eyes but sometimes he'd scan the room with a questioning expression. After a few minutes, he craned to see and hear what was going on around him. I worried about breaking the rhythm. His head felt awkward and as heavy as a bowling ball. I couldn't understand why I'd been directed to hold his head instead of an arm or a leg. Even then, I thought one of the adults should have had Jimmy's head. It would become clear to me later why they didn't want the lead responsibility. If I didn't set the pace correctly, then only I was to blame.

This way. That way. My palms sweated and slipped on Jimmy's skin. I felt a dull pop from his ear when my cupped hand momentarily lost control of his head. Unsure what to do, I winced at the other patterners in a plea for help. They only nodded indicating I should keep going, keep the pace.

Well . . . maybe I can do this. Yes, I think I can. I can do this. I can be in charge. I am in charge. Flip. Flap. Flip. Flap.

I kept wondering why Jimmy's brain was different from mine. In my young brain, I asked what happened inside his skull when I moved his head side to side. Did his brain squish back and forth against the bone? Flip. Flap. Would he be able to speak more clearly soon? Flip. Flap. I thought if I took the lead patterner role more often, maybe he'd get better faster because I was his sister. Flip. Flap. And then Mom would be happy. Flip Flap. The head was the most important part of the body and it was in my hands. How . . . much longer . . . do I . . . have to . . . do this?

Even though Jimmy was the special member of our family, I began to feel special too, but in a different way. I felt like a grown-up. Because I had performed an adult responsibility, I expected my mother would ask me to pattern more often.

Ding! The session ended.

Climbing the stairs among the adults after that first patterning session, I couldn't have known I had been permanently thrust out of my childhood and into adulthood, while my dear brother

Jimmy, with very special needs, remained in a lonely, innocent world. It's a world I've been struggling ever since to understand.

The little patterner, age 5

For two years we patterned Jimmy, two shifts a day, every day: mid-morning with the neighborhood moms and nighttime after dinner with mostly fathers. Each shift consisted of two segments lasting five minutes with a half-hour break in between.

On Saturday mornings, Matthew Clark often came along with his mother. During the break, he'd lie down on the floor of our small living room and rest his head on a sofa pillow propped against the wall. Jimmy would cuddle next to Matthew who read aloud from his newest comic books.

Matthew transported Jimmy to a land of wonder, where

troubles were erased in seconds. Matthew held Jimmy's attention, reading from Superman and Batman. Matthew's voice got stronger like a TV actor. He'd point to the mysterious, muscular hero in a colorful skin-tight leotard and eye mask who, with super-human skills, jumped from rooftops and swooshed down from tall buildings to knock out the bad guy and rescue the damsel in distress.

"Pow!" "Ka-put!" "Wham!"

Jimmy was in awe. He'd sit there with his mouth open, saliva dripping from his lower lip. Through his thick eyeglasses, he stared at Matthew in amazement. Matthew's head was practically in between the pages of the comic book. He was so absorbed that I think he often forgot Jimmy was sitting next to him. Matthew must have imagined being a superhero. I wonder if Jimmy knew the difference between the comic book characters and real life people.

Matthew befriended Jimmy in a way nobody else had until then. He read to Jimmy who trusted every word he spoke. If Matthew mispronounced a word, it didn't matter because Jimmy couldn't discern it. It didn't matter if Matthew might have had a limited vocabulary compared to other kids his age who may have read fat chapter books without pictures. Matthew calmed my brother after a grueling week of patterning. I could tell Jimmy was relaxed because his whole body sunk into itself. For a brief, fantastical time, Matthew acted like Jimmy's big brother. Matthew would never know how much he helped Jimmy learn and grow.

"See ya next Saturday, Jimmy," Matthew would say as he rolled over onto his hands and knees, collected his comic books and lugged himself upright.

"Bye," said Jimmy with a half smile and a wave, still seated cross-legged on the floor.

After two years, the patterning stopped.

"I think you started too late," Dr. Spitz concluded.

I never saw my parents express outrage or disappointment. They wanted to believe their emotional, physical, and financial investment paid off, even if they couldn't prove it scientifically–a belief I can easily understand after becoming a parent myself.

Almost twenty years after we stopped patterning Jimmy, the American Academy of Pediatrics concluded the treatment had no discernable effect on children with brain damage and that any claims by its advocates were unproven.

Nor has there been much to support the medical value of another exercise the doctor taught my parents, concurrent with the patterning, called "masking." Dr. Spitz convinced my parents to put a plastic bag over Jimmy's head and tie it under his chin twice a day for a minute each episode. The theory was that inhaling carbon dioxide would automatically increase blood flow to the brain as the body's way of responding to the risk of suffocation. The neurosurgeon compared it to the fight or flight experience of a firefighter.

The practice seemed barbaric but my parents were not ones to question a doctor. They reasoned the doctor must have known what to do since he was formally educated with multiple degrees. It pained my parents to put the mask over Jimmy's head and watch their little boy struggle. But they'd do anything if they thought it would help their son. After a month of masking, my parents finally trusted their instincts and stopped the "exercise."

Even to this day, I find it hard to understand what the patterning, masking, and other exercises might have achieved from a medical point of view. My parents and their closest friends believed the patterning did work because they observed Jimmy become more talkative and confident. His eye contact improved. He showed more interest in playing games and he grew physically stronger. Whether he would have made these behavioral changes without the patterning, we'd never know.

What I do know is that love trumps science. I believe what truly made all the difference in Jimmy's development was the abundance of love and support he received. When the patterning ended, all the neighbors chipped in and bought Jimmy a bicycle. And they continued to look out for him. To witness a community rally around him the way they did, to feel the love of my extended family, to hear the laughter of Mom and Dad's friends in our home is a joy every child seeks.

As a little girl, I knew Jimmy was the needy one but I yearned for some attention like he received from the volunteers. That wouldn't happen. I'd have to get used to being on the sidelines. To hearing "Jimmy and Joyce," never "Joyce and Jimmy." To seeing Mom's eyes directed to Jimmy first whenever she entered the room.

My parents, the hopeful newlyweds
Philadelphia, Pennsylvania
May 4, 1952

3

After my first assignment as lead patterner, I never played with dolls again. Over time, the hours of my life became filled with the job of being Jimmy's sister: walking to and from school with him, making sure his coat was buttoned properly, helping him with homework, teaching him how to make his bed. I naturally considered it my assigned station in life and wanted to please Mom and Dad by performing the job well.

One afternoon I was sitting on the porch steps reading when I heard hollering. The neighborhood boys were playing cowboys and Indians. I turned my head in the direction of the next twin house and saw Jimmy being tied to the trunk of a maple tree. I leaped from the steps and ran across the lawn toward the commotion, thinking: *My brother! That's my brother!*

Christopher Terranova laughed as he ran around the tree, wrapping Jimmy tightly to the trunk with a clothesline. The other boys yelled wildly and shot off their cap guns while Jimmy chuckled. I couldn't determine if it was one of his nervous laughs or a genuine one. I pleaded with Christopher to let Jimmy go.

"Get out of the way!" Christopher yelled, elbowing me to the side. He kept running around the tree, an evil grin on his face.

"Gimme!" I said, grabbing the rope. As a second-grader, I wasn't strong enough to pull the rope away from Christopher who almost knocked me to the ground. I stumbled backwards and worried if he would tie me up next. I stared at Jimmy and felt pity for him, but he continued laughing. His arms were pinned against the tree trunk, the clothesline wrapped around him from shoulders to feet. His head whipped from side to side trying to follow Christopher.

"Go away, Joyce!" Jimmy demanded. He'd outgrown the Goy-kee by now.

I hoped somebody's mom would peek out a window and come to Jimmy's rescue. I debated whether to tell Mom. If I told, then she might ask me why I left Jimmy tied up, and I hadn't an answer. There was also a chance Mrs. Terranova, Christopher's mom, would stop coming to our house to visit Mom and I didn't want that to happen.

I knew they had singled Jimmy out as an easy target and were taunting him. Still, he enjoyed the attention. Unlike me, he'd found a natural way to fit in. It wasn't common for girls to be physically active back then the way boys were, always tossing a ball or running around. Girls were supposed to play with Barbie dolls and Easy Bake Ovens. None of that interested me, so I found myself alone and confused.

Although I figured Jimmy wouldn't really be injured, I felt embarrassed and helpless. It would be one of many times I tried to protect and defend Jimmy. Walking backward, I left the boys to their antics wondering how long they'd leave him like that.

I took my book and sauntered to the backyard alone.

There weren't any girls my age on the street, so I tagged along with my sister Lynne, four years older, and her friend Christine Verdi, whenever they let me. I wished I had been the oldest because it seemed like Lynne could do whatever she wanted. She always got to do things first and better, like use the pink hair curlers or sit by the window in the new Dodge Dart. The only time I wasn't jealous of Lynne was on Christmas morning when she was last in the line-up to go downstairs.

"Can I come?" I'd ask squeezing my legs together because I had to pee again.

"Joyce, if you have to go to the bathroom, then go. We'll wait for you," Lynne would say. Then she and Christine would ditch me by the time I returned.

Occasionally, they included me in games of Mother May I, Red Light/Green Light, and hopscotch with the other kids on the block. They let me go with them to Fariston Hill. That's where we'd put a fat, yellow phone book on top of a metal roller skate (the kind you clip on to your shoes), sit on top of the book, stick our feet up in the air and go rolling down the hill. I'd watch with envy as Lynne and Christine laughed all the way to the bottom while I'd struggle alone on the asphalt.

Often I'd read *The Bobbsey Twins* or wander to the backyard. Mom hung the laundry on the clothesline back there. It was directly outside our basement door, a few steps from the washing machine.

"Be careful not to dirty the bed sheets," she'd call from the kitchen window overlooking the alley.

Later in the afternoon, the temptation to run through the crisp, white sheets flapping against each other in the gentle breeze was too great. I noticed the clothespin marks at the top corners of the sheets that Mom would smooth out when she folded them later. Hidden between the sheets, I put my nose close enough to inhale the clean detergent and caress the cold stiffness with my hands. There I could be invisible, wrapped among the freshly washed linens. That pursuit of invisibility intrigued me as a child and would again in my teens and adulthood.

Beyond the clothesline ran an alley wide enough for a car. Between the alley and the creek lay a tiny yard about the size of two parking spaces where Dad used the old push mower and Mom planted marigolds. In late afternoons, she'd take her cigarettes out there and sit in a metal lawn chair smoking and chatting with Aunt Anna or another neighbor.

"I know I should quit but cigarettes are my friend," Mom repeated throughout the years. Even after all of her friends and relatives quit smoking, she continued. She acted predictably, smoking with her morning coffee, after meals, in the backyard, and in her car. The only room in the house where she smoked was the kitchen, or the dining room after a holiday meal. She never smoked in the living room or upstairs. She was fastidious about her smoking routine, putting the butts and ashes in a coffee can with a lid on it under the sink.

"Mom, why don't you try to quit like Aunt Anna did?" I asked several times.

"Smoking calms me," she said, exhaling a puff. "Besides, it's my only vice."

Growing up, every night after dinner, she'd ask me to bring her pack of Kent cigarettes and an ashtray to the table. I hated doing it, hated the smell and smoke, and couldn't understand how she could follow a delicious meal with nicotine. Even when my friends and sisters took up smoking in their twenties, I never did.

I pleaded with my mother after Dad's heart surgery when he was seventy-eight.

"Mom, you're an intelligent woman," I said. "You know all the health risks associated with smoking."

"This relaxes me, Joyce," she'd say with finality, extending the cigarette toward me. Then she'd rest her hands on the chair with the smoke billowing from between her fingers and stare into the garden with a faraway look. "It's a burden that never goes away," she'd say without turning her head. After I'd become a mother myself and Jimmy aged into his thirties and beyond, she'd repeat this more often. I'd always wait for her to continue. She'd shake her head as if to forget her troubles. She wanted me to know about the increasing difficulty taking care of Jimmy but, at the same time, didn't want me to shoulder more than I had to.

I knew she always worried about Jimmy—about whether he'd adapt to a new school or environment and make friends. Her brows were knit and the lines in her forehead deepened. She wrung her hands a lot. Would people be kind to him? Would he get a job and be able to live independently?

Those same questions and more still haunt me today. Is Jimmy safe? Will he watch his sugar intake and manage his diabetes? Will he follow the rules established by his doctors and social workers at the supervised apartment where he lives? The refrain always echoed in my mind and became louder with each passing year.

Even as a kid, I worried about Jimmy. Yet he was more successful than I was in finding friends and playing in the neighborhood. Boys like the Morettos and Verdis dominated the scene. I'd made friends with Karen and Cheryl but then they moved away so I tagged along with my sister Lynne and her friends when they'd let me.

I don't know how long Jimmy remained tied to that tree. I'm sure he never gave it a second thought but the image of him helpless and taunted has never left me.

4

When it came time to enroll Jimmy in school, St. Bernadette's wasn't an option because they didn't offer a special education class. Jimmy had had a number of tests to assess his cognitive abilities. His IQ was sixty-eight, a number Dr. Spitz defined as "borderline educable."

If Jimmy had been born in 1976 instead of 1956 I'm convinced he would have progressed significantly more. In the 1960s there were fewer resources, and worse, fewer expectations, for children with disabilities. In fact, children like Jimmy did not even have the right to a public education. In 1971, the Pennsylvania Association for Retarded Children (PARC) filed a lawsuit against the Commonwealth of Pennsylvania seeking to overturn the law. The case settled and resulted in a decree requiring the state to provide a free public education to all children with mental retardation. It became the basis for the right for all children with intellectual disabilities. It further stated that children should have an individualized education and be placed in the least restrictive environment possible. In 1975, the consent decree was codified on a national level with the congressional passing of Public Law 94-142, the Education for All Handicapped Children Act, now known as the Individuals with Disabilities Education Act (IDEA).

Children like my brother remained in society's shadows until Eunice Shriver became their advocate and brought them into the sunlight. Inspired by her older sister who was born with intellectual disabilities, Eunice urged her brother, President John F. Kennedy, to prioritize care and support for citizens like Jimmy. One month before he was assassinated, on October 24, 1963, the president signed the Maternal and Child Health and Mental Retardation Planning Amendment to the Social Security Act. It was the first major legislation to address what was then called mental retardation, and it paved the way for more attention and support to a marginalized community. Eunice worked tirelessly her whole life for the rights of these special citizens. Perhaps her greatest legacy is the founding of Special Olympics in 1968. My mother credited the pioneering, indomitable Mrs. Shriver for single-handedly creating opportunities for people with disabilities.

But at the time, few, if any, rights were available for Jimmy. So instead of attending St. Bernadette's with Lynne, Jimmy started public school with me at Hillcrest Elementary. That September, he was six and I was four—always among the youngest in my class with a November birthday.

School became my refuge. It took me away from the responsibilities of home. By mid-August every year, I'd be itching to return to the classroom.

"Mom, can we go to Bond's and shop for school supplies?" I wanted to assemble my looseleaf paper and dividers in a binder and put Bic pens and yellow Ticonderoga pencils in a zippered pencil case.

"Let's wait for school to start," she'd say. With an eye on the family budget, she likely wanted to see exactly what supplies the teachers required instead of overspending in advance.

In the classroom, I immersed myself in reading, learning and searching for answers to problems. I was happily untethered and alone—a boat sailing in a sea of knowledge. I admired my teachers and thought I'd become one someday. Being a student was the first role I took on other than Jimmy's sister. It gave me a kernel of freedom to be in a room without him.

My second grade teacher was from the South. Mrs. Hayes was all business—tough, strict and rarely with a smile. She favored plaid dresses belted tightly at the waist on her tall, skinny frame. Her wavy brown hair had streaks of gray and she wore cat-eye glasses. At least once a day, she'd call on a student I still hadn't met.

"Idy Claire!" she'd say, shaking her head, when no one responded to a question.

Who was Idy Claire? I'd scan the first floor classroom waiting for someone to respond.

"Idy Claire!" she'd yell on the playground when trying to round up all the kids to return indoors. I continued to search for this new student. Mrs. Hayes called this girl's name whenever she was frustrated or wanted immediate attention such as "Idy Claire, Bobby! Pay attention!"

One particular afternoon I found myself frustrated and ready to invoke Idy Claire's name. It happened at the end of the school day when Mrs. Hayes was reading a story to us. She paused and asked, "Who would like to read aloud to the class today?" I flapped my hand in the air "ooh-oohing" with the other students desperate for a chance, yet I knew perfectly well Mrs. Hayes would select Wendy Norbert again.

The time neared three o'clock and Wendy had her head between the pages reading loud and fast, barely taking a breath. I had a hard time staying with her story because I had to pee.

The waistband of my skirt dug into my belly. I didn't think I could make it until the three o'clock bell, so I raised my hand to ask Mrs. Hayes if I could be excused to go to the bathroom. Mrs. Hayes remained seated and ignored me. I stretched my right hand higher and waved my fingertips. While leaning forward, my left hand gripped the front corner of the desk. My thighs squeezed together with my knees barely crossing over each other. Mrs. Hayes still refused to acknowledge me. I became so frustrated that I wanted to shout, "Idy Claire, Mrs. Hayes! I really, really have to go." My bladder was ready to burst. But students were not allowed to get up from their seats without Mrs. Hayes's permission and I always followed the rules.

My hand slowly lowered. A trickle made its way down both legs. The hot urine quickly saturated my navy blue leotards. The back of my wool skirt moistened. After my initial relief, humiliation set in. I prayed no one noticed and I kept still, doodling to avoid eye contact with anyone. When the bell finally rang, I grabbed my coat and headed for the door.

I found Jimmy in the special education classroom. We pushed open the heavy school doors to the fresh air outside and began our walk home together. Jimmy never noticed I had peed myself and I was too embarrassed to tell him. Now it was I who did something that wasn't age appropriate. I feared a boy in the schoolyard might point at me, laugh and sing: "*Baby, baby, stick your head in gravy. Don't take it out til you're in the Navy.*" Jimmy would never tease me that way. He stayed right by my side making me feel safe. He guarded me without knowing it.

My plaid kilt and bulky winter coat covered most of the soaked leotards. My legs became sticky and the leotard started to stiffen from the cold weather. I had a tough time waddling down the street, forced to shuffle my feet side to side instead of one in front of the other.

On the way home, I tried to anticipate Mom's reaction and wondered if she'd put a plastic liner on my bed like she did on Jimmy's. She changed his sheets more than once a week whenever he wet the bed. At least he hadn't mortified himself by peeing his pants in the classroom.

Stepping into the house, I wrinkled my nose at the odor between my legs. There was no way to avoid Mom. I could barely look her in the eye.

"I had an accident," I said with my head lowered. "Mrs. Hayes wouldn't let me go to the bathroom." I wanted to cry but struggled to avoid more baby behavior.

"Go upstairs, take off all your clothes and throw them in the hamper," she said calmly. "Wash yourself with soap and water. Then put on new underwear and your play clothes. When you're done, come downstairs."

I returned to our living room to see Mom waiting for me on the sofa.

"Joycie," she said taking my hands in hers, "do you feel better now?"

I nodded, my head still lowered.

Then she placed her warm fingertips under my chin and tilted my head up. Her gentle smile relaxed me.

"Honey, why didn't you get up from your seat and go to the bathroom?"

"How could I without Mrs. Hayes's permission?" I replied. "It's her rules."

"Sweetheart . . . occasionally, it's okay not to follow the rules."

Mom couldn't have known her phrase would reverberate for years. I don't think she meant that it was okay to forge her signature on my "D" geometry test or to steal Peanut Chews from the Aronimink Pharmacy where I worked. Nor would she have condoned the one time I hitchhiked with some girls in high school just to go along with the crowd. I'd told my parents that we planned to walk to the school dance when suddenly Cindy stuck out her thumb. I was petrified that a neighbor or uncle would see me and tell Mom and Dad. That scared me more than getting into the car with a stranger for the half-mile ride down State Road.

As the daughter who always endeavored to comply, Mom couldn't have imagined that I'd later ignore a few rules while pursuing a career in the emerging, male-dominated field of technology. I'd have to assert myself on several occasions to ensure my salary remained competitive. Moreover, I'd eagerly advocate for competent women to be recognized and promoted into management positions when the male decision-makers hadn't given it a second thought.

"David," I asked a vice president one morning in a staff meeting. "Week after week you praise Kathleen and tell us how much the customers love her. When are you going to promote her?" It was tremendously gratifying for me to have had a hand in leveling the playing field in a business setting and to see talented women advance.

5

After the wet leotard incident, I became more aware of my age. "I'm the youngest person in my class," I complained to Mom.

"So was I," she said. By the end of her first grade, the nuns at St. Donato's had convinced my grandmother to allow Mom to skip second grade and go directly to third grade. "I was twelve years old when I entered ninth grade at West Catholic Girls' High and sixteen when I graduated. That's why I started smoking . . . so I would look older." The cigarette habit she started as a young teen continued for more than sixty years.

Mom grew up in a disciplined home and learned even more discipline at St. Donato's and West Catholic High in Philadelphia. She often talked about the strict requirements of the all-girls high school where classrooms burgeoned with up to sixty students. She applied the adherence to rules and learning to her own children and to managing the home.

Wednesday mornings before leaving for school, I'd often turn at the front door and plead with Mom, "Do I still have to go to Catechism? I never learn anything there." I'd do anything to avoid that hike to St. Bernadette's. Its boxy brick building was dark and cold inside.

"Yes, you have to go," she'd reply. "It's important so you and Jimmy can make your first holy communion. Those are the rules."

"But it's the same thing every week! The only thing the nuns do is repeat Jesus loves us. They write JOY on the blackboard, with the O under the J and the Y under the O to explain what is important in life." I mimicked writing in the space between Mom and me. "They say 'J' is for Jesus, who comes first, 'O' is for Others, who come second, and 'Y' is for You, who comes last. I know it already and so does Jimmy."

"Well, you still have to go." She put her hands on my shoulders, turned me around, and shooed me out.

I stomped down the front steps and reminded myself to invent another excuse by the following week. Truthfully, I couldn't figure out who Jesus was. I didn't understand who God was. And I certainly had no clue about the stranger known as the Holy Ghost. How could a ghost be scary and holy at the same time?

So instead of walking home on Wednesday afternoons after the three o'clock school bell rang, Jimmy and I plodded six blocks in the other direction to St. Bernadette's School for an hour of Catechism. We hated it. By the time class ended at four-thirty we were starved, and we still had to trek another twelve blocks home.

St. Bernadette's School was stark and colorless compared to Hillcrest Elementary. The nuns dressed in funereal black, the bulletin boards remained undecorated, and all the statues and crucifixes stared down at us. Even though the nuns taught us the word "catholic" meant universal and said the Catholic Church welcomed everyone, it never felt that way to me.

"The nuns don't like us public school kids," I said to Mom, putting my Catechism book on the dining room table.

"Why do you say that?"

"Because they're always angry with us. They never smile. All they do is tell us to form a straight line and pray."

The nuns appeared ultra-organized in the classroom with their Palmer penmanship cards across the top of the blackboards and clickers in hand. The clicker was nothing but a wooden clothespin with a spring. They'd snap, snap, snap the clicker to get our attention or to call the classroom to order. They were intoxicated with power using the clicker.

The Sisters of Notre Dame wore floor-length black dresses. I couldn't figure out why they were called habits. I'd been taught habits were things you couldn't stop—like Mom couldn't stop smoking. They also sported a wimple—a starched, white cloth used to cover their head and neck all the way to their chin. No wonder they always had their noses in the air; they couldn't tilt their chins down because their white accordion neckerchief fit too tightly. Under the wimple, the white fabric mounted across their forehead was stiff enough to indent the skin above their brow. I wondered if all that tightness gave them headaches. Did they wrap their hair in a French twist, like Mom, before putting on the wimple, or was their hair cut very short in a pixie? I never saw any bobby pins and couldn't figure out how those holy headpieces stayed on their heads. And the starchy, oversized white collar that looked like a bib. Did they ever drip gravy on it when they ate spaghetti? I was curious to know if they had extras or only one that they hand-washed in the bathroom sink every night and then hung over the shower rod to dry.

Rosary beads draped from their waists and, at the end of the chain, a cross dangled by their knees. The chain of beads swung when they walked, peeking in and out of the folds of their habit. Besides sensible old-lady shoes, I wondered if they wore a lace slip and nylon stockings with a garter belt under those long, shrouded habits. Or if they knotted thick support stockings at the knee like Grandmom did. Whenever a nun put her hands into what appeared to be a secret pocket at her waist, I wondered if she was trying to keep warm like I did with my white muff or if she was reaching to grab that ridiculous clicker and yell at us again.

All the second-graders plus Jimmy, one year ahead of me, were getting ready to make our first holy communion. The nuns didn't spend as much time preparing us for the confessional as they did preparing us to receive the Host. We learned the Host was also known as the Eucharist, the Body of Christ, the Bread of Life, and the communion wafer.

"Why are there so many names for one thing?" I asked Mom one day after Catechism. I'd been too scared to question the nuns in class. I figured the Host's off-white color suggested it would taste like a Nabisco vanilla wafer, my favorite flavor.

"I don't know, that's the way I learned it, too," she said leaning over the kitchen sink.

The nuns taught us to kneel at the metal railing before the altar and respond "Amen" when the monsignor presented us with the Eucharist while saying "The Body of Christ." Then we were to stick out our tongue for the priest to place the Host. Never, ever, under any circumstances, were we to touch the wafer with our hand. Nor were we to chew it or part our lips. Furthermore, if the wafer got stuck on the roof of our mouth, we were to use our tongue to scrape it from our palate and then moisten it enough to swallow. What was this wafer made of anyway? It didn't look like bread to me. If bread was being offered, I preferred Amoroso's crusty Italian style.

Finally, I'd see behind those burgundy velvet curtains at

the back of the church. Being near the confessional gave me the heebie-jeebies. It reminded me of the secret place where The Wizard of Oz hid, fooling everybody. I reached on top of my head to secure the bobby pin to my white chapel veil. It resembled one of Mom's doilies she used for holiday desserts. I yearned for a long chapel veil like Lynne's.

In the darkness of the confessional the size of a coat closet, my young hands balled into fists. As the curtain drooped, the air grew tight around me. With baby steps, I inched my way to the kneeler, hitting it with the tip of my shoe. I lowered myself and waited. Mom would have washed away the musty, woodsy odor with Pine Sol. I wondered who could see me. I thought there was a chance someone could be hiding behind a secret door or spying on me from a hole in the ceiling. There wasn't even a ledge to rest my hands, folded in prayer. I heard movements on the other side of the wall. For all I knew, it could have been the Holy Ghost. I banged the heels of my shoes together while waiting. Then I jerked to attention at the sound of the little door sliding open leaving me facing a metal screen and a shadowy figure on the other side.

"Bless me Father, for I have sinned, this is my first confession," I said with bowed head as instructed. My bony knees stuck to the vinyl-cushioned kneeler. I hadn't determined what sins I'd report to this strange man who I could not see. I hadn't stolen or lied or done anything bad so I debated whether to make something up.

I wondered how Jimmy would manage himself in the confessional. Would he remember what to do? It was going to be difficult for him to memorize "Bless me Father, for I have sinned, this is my first confession" because the phrase contained more words than he could memorize. If I couldn't think of a sin I committed, surely he couldn't either. I prayed whichever priest Jimmy got would be compassionate–a priest who'd be able to quickly ascertain Jimmy's special needs and let him off the hook with a simple blessing. If he got a priest who insisted on formality, then I imagined Jimmy stammering, "I don't know" or "I don't remember." We'd find out later what happened before Jimmy was dismissed from the confessional.

"What sins have you committed?" the faceless priest asked me in a monotone voice.

Committed? I thought. That was a word used with criminals on the evening news. I hadn't committed anything. All those instructions from the nuns and I was still unprepared.

The priest waited without even giving me a hint. A few seconds of awkward silence passed.

"I talked back to my parents," I blurted. Although my parents set an expectation never to talk back to anyone, I had felt pressured to say something. Suddenly, without thinking of the consequences, I'd created a situation and lied to the priest. Guilt pangs arose at the thought of Mom and Dad discovering their daughter simultaneously lying to a priest and hinting at family conflict. Had I committed a sin in the confessional? Would I burn in hell? The situation kept getting worse. Dear God, I prayed, please get me out of this musty-smelling closet.

"Anything else?"

What did this strange man want to hear?

"Um, no."

"Well then, it's important to obey and respect your parents at all times. I want you to say three Our Fathers and three Hail Marys as your penance. You may go."

He slid the door closed in my face without a goodbye or a thank you. As if priests were exempt from good manners.

They didn't appear human to me. You couldn't touch them. They didn't wear everyday clothing like my father. And what really bothered me was their insistence in being addressed as "Father." I had my own father who would give the priests a piece of his mind more than once over the years.

All those Catechism classes and I barely spent a minute in the confessional. I put my hands on the wall for balance and rose from the kneeler. Then I pivoted right, reached for the velvet curtain, and held it for the next victim. Spots floated in front of my eyes as they adjusted to the church lights while I made the long, guilty walk to the metal altar railing to say my penance.

We practiced our procession from the school to the church, paired alphabetically in double file lines. Boys led and girls followed. Dear God, I prayed, please don't place me next to Kathy Patterson, the ugly girl in class with body odor. Surely Kathy didn't bathe or wash her hair regularly. The Lord didn't listen to my prayer. I heard Sister Theresa, who talked with a lisp and possessed the disgusting habit of forming bubbles at the corner of her mouth, call "Patterson" followed by "Poggi" to team up as partners. Apparently, Kathy didn't remember the Catechism lesson that cleanliness is next to godliness. Instead of showing compassion for Kathy, who clearly came from a poor family, I concerned myself with the bad luck of getting assigned to walk next to her. I worried the angelic dress my godmother made for me would get dirty if it brushed up against Kathy, and her odor would drift my way.

It had never occurred to me that a second grade boy probably had the same emotional reaction toward Jimmy that I had toward Kathy Patterson. What "normal" boy would have wanted to be paired with my brother who was developmentally slow? People avoided my brother the same way I tried to avoid Kathy. Jimmy didn't possess the social agility of other kids his age or even younger and he didn't have the benefits of any of the familiar neighborhood boys in his Catechism class. I had been too young to embrace and practice the Catholic teachings of inclusion by befriending Kathy in the hopes of Jimmy's classmates doing the same.

Jimmy and I finished our last practice at Catechism class and made the long, block-after-block walk home, knowing the next time we attended church, we'd finally make our first holy communion. He'd wear the new suit and tie Mom bought and I'd be a vision of white in my new dress, lace hairband with attached veil, and patent leather shoes.

Fifty years later I found out what happened the night before my first holy communion. I was visiting Dad after Mom had died. He recollected stories of his parents, his Army days, Mom and, of course, Jimmy. Even in his old age, most of the stories about Jimmy rattled Dad with regret, anger, and what could have been.

"The telephone rang," Dad told me. "After a short conversation, your mother hung up and walked from the kitchen to the living room with a blank expression on her face. I asked her what was wrong. She said Father Murphy had called to say Jimmy couldn't make his first holy communion the next day."

"I never knew that, Dad," I said.

"It's true. He said because Jimmy didn't know what to say in the confession box, Monsignor O'Brien decided Jimmy couldn't receive communion. Can you imagine?" Dad said, shaking his head side to side. "Your mother was crying."

"What happened?"

"I grabbed my keys and drove to the rectory. Father Murphy met me in the hallway and then Sister Superior showed up. I asked them why Jimmy couldn't make his first holy communion. 'Jimmy can be in the procession,' Father Murphy said, 'but he'll have to receive an unconsecrated host.'"

"I yelled at him. 'What?' I said. 'I can give him graham crackers at home!'"

Despite my father's anger, I couldn't resist a laugh. The image of him yelling "graham crackers" in a place I had found stale and intimidating was a relief.

"And that Sister Superior . . . she kept bowing her head with her hands in prayer saying, 'God will provide, Mr. Poggi. God will provide.' I turned to her and said 'What's that supposed to mean?' And she kept repeating, 'God will provide. God will provide.'"

"Then what happened?"

"I told them I wanted to talk to Monsignor O'Brien but they told me he was unavailable. Do you believe that?" he asked shaking his head again. "So I leaned in and said, 'You tell the monsignor Jimmy *will* make his first holy communion tomorrow—with a consecrated host. Remind him Jimmy fulfilled all the requirements of the Church like all the other children.'"

I pictured my father's confrontation and felt proud. It was unheard of for anyone to challenge the Catholic Church. Priests presented themselves as untouchable, but Dad's paternal and moral instincts were stronger than Catholic protocol.

"Before I left the rectory, I let them have it. I pointed right at them." He wagged his finger to illustrate and continued, "I told them, 'My son Jimmy, more than any other Catechism student, is a very special child of God. And *you*, of all people, should know better.'"

The following morning Jimmy made his sacrament with a consecrated host with me and the other children. The wafer tasted like cardboard and, of course, got stuck on the roof of my mouth. After the ceremony, we posed for the obligatory family photos outside the church under serene May skies in front of the statue of the Virgin Mary.

Our first holy communion day
Drexel Hill, Pennsylvania
May, 1965

When we returned home, Dad slammed the car door.

"That damn monsignor!" he said walking briskly toward the front door with us trailing behind him. "Why can't he pronounce the Italian names?" he asked, raising both hands. "What's so hard about Poggi and DiCanzio? He has no trouble pronouncing McAnally and O'Leary," Dad harrumphed.

Almost overnight, Mom and Dad developed a different perspective on their religion. They decided to transfer Lynne from St. Bernadette's to the public junior high school in September. After being taught never to challenge the Catholic Church, now they questioned everything about it, forever altered by the experience.

After our sacramental day, our family attended mass only occasionally instead of every Sunday. When we did go, we prayed Dad would reward us for our obedience by driving to Montbard's Bakery for Persians. Persians were enormous pastries—heavy, buttery dough rolled in a circle of cinnamon with a thick slab of either a rich chocolate or creamy vanilla frosting on top. I prayed for Persians during mass.

Twenty years after our first holy communion, our parish served up another injustice. Mom repeated this chapter of our family lore to me several times, too. She heard the doorbell ring and answered the front door.

"Hello, Mrs. Poggi. I'm Father Dougherty, the new priest at St. Bernadette's. I noticed by reviewing the parish census you haven't been attending mass. May I talk to you about re-engaging with the church?"

Catholic guilt swelled in my mother. She reluctantly welcomed the young priest into her home. She and Dad sat in the living room and listened to the priest talk about parish programs.

"What can St. Bernadette's do for you?" asked the priest.

Mom paused for a moment. She couldn't believe a representative of the church was sitting in her living room asking what he could do for her instead of being asked what she could do for the church. She decided to take a risk.

"My son Jimmy needs a job. It's important to my husband and me that Jimmy be a contributing member of society. Is there part-time work at St. Bernadette's for him?" she asked with traces of hope and humility. "Custodial or cafeteria work? Or maybe a social group for Jimmy you could recommend?"

"We couldn't possibly do that," the priest answered without missing a beat.

It only took Mom a few seconds to rise from the couch and politely escort the priest to the door. Dad lowered his head and shook it from side to side, unsurprised.

From that point forward, Mom and Dad stopped attending mass, except for funerals, weddings, and baptisms. Mom insisted she was as spiritual as ever, if not more. She abided by God's law instead of the Catholic Church's law and she continued to pray every day. She said she felt closest to God when she was on her knees digging in her garden.

After all the lessons about the Catholic Church being an open community where everyone is welcome, all I remember is they rejected Jimmy.

6

Thirty-five years after his first holy communion, in January of the year 2000, Jimmy finally found a warm welcome outside his immediate family. At age forty-three he was the first resident in a supervised apartment complex. The three-story building offered several units for special needs adults and the rest of the apartments were reserved for senior citizens. (In preparation for his move to semi-independent living, Jimmy had gone on occasional respite weekends in the homes of social workers for a couple of years leading up to the move. This arrangement gave both my parents and my brother time to adjust to living apart from each other.)

Jimmy was apprehensive but cooperative. He kept saying, "I want to come home." He asked why he couldn't continue living with Mom and Dad. They explained that he had to develop independence because they would likely die before him. He asked why he couldn't live with one of his sisters.

"Because Lynne, Joyce and Alison have their own families. They have to take care of their children." Jimmy asked a few more times the following year and then dropped the idea when he saw there was no traction.

"Jimmy, look at this brand new building," Mom said, trying her best to encourage him. "You're going to have your own apartment and make new friends." That wouldn't come easily since he had been mainstreamed for most of his early adult life. He'd consistently accompanied my parents on trips and dinner dates with their friends who were always welcoming and conversational with Jimmy.

Now he had to connect with individuals of lesser intellectual ability than him. He considered himself stronger, mentally and physically, than the other special needs adults moving into the complex. Often, he was more capable. Therefore he resisted engaging with someone who didn't speak clearly or who used crutches, because they slowed Jimmy down, and that frustrated him. He often kept to himself. However, he did like earning money by working part-time at a grocery store, collecting carts and sweeping the entrance. He liked the side benefits of easy access to sweets and soda, too.

Instead of respites in other people's homes, Jimmy's weekend retreats would occur at my parents' house. My father would make the forty-five minute commute to pick him up and take him back.

As difficult as it was for Jimmy, it was equally if not more difficult for my mother. Soon after he moved out, she fell into a depression and her physical health began its long decline. She suffered severe headaches, a stroke, and heart disease along with a roster of other ailments. She socialized very little and spent most of the day on the couch. Every time I encouraged her to go for a walk or get exercise, she sighed and said, "I'm too tired."

As a result of Mom's failing health, I began to step in when issues with Jimmy arose. He experienced behavioral swings caused by any number of things: anxiety about an upcoming holiday, his desire for more money, a broken watch, hunger, an annoying roommate. I received lots of calls from the social workers: Jimmy's not cooperating, he leaves the building without telling us, we're worried about his personal safety, he's not attentive when crossing the street, his eating is out of control, his sugar level is sky high. One time I met him in the hospital emergency room after driving five and a half hours in a thunderstorm only to hear him tell me his stomach hurt. Doctors ran tests, prescribed meds, told him to stick to a sugar-free diet and sent him home. Finally, when I was notified that he threw a chair and barricaded himself in his bedroom, I knew a change had to happen.

"It's the meds. He's on the wrong meds," I said to the staff supervisor. Jimmy could be ornery now and then but my brother was never violent. I reviewed his medication list and discovered one doctor prescribed an anti-psychotic along with the anti-depressant. "Jimmy is depressed. He's not psychotic. I know my brother," I said keeping a strong, even-toned voice.

Abilify curbed his appetite, reduced his blood sugar level and worked for six months. Geodon made him belligerent. Latuda made him zombie-like. He'd stopped calling his sisters. He barely spoke and when he did, he gave one-word answers. When Lynne and I took him to buy new bedroom furniture, we hardly recognized him. He had vacant eyes, a clenched jaw, sweated profusely, and his equilibrium was off. He tiptoed with a cautious gait and raised his arms out to either side to balance himself. He wore the same dingy clothes, slept a lot, hadn't participated in social events, never smiled, and didn't hug back.

"That's not my brother, " I said to the social worker privately in the staff office. "What happened?" I asked, standing at the corner of her desk.

"Well," she said, seated, with a forced smile, "he's not

complaining about his stomach anymore."

I was shocked by this comment from someone who had provided genuine support to Jimmy. I wanted to say, *Sure, as long as he's making your life easier, you're glad to keep him in a near-comatose state.* Despite rising anger, I kept my cool. It was important for me to maintain open and constructive relationships with the social workers. After all, they were taking care of Jimmy.

"I want my brother back. Please let his doctor know I want to talk to him as soon as possible."

Several times I'd be on the phone with Jimmy and ask him how he was doing.

"I take too much medicine. Too many pills. I don't like it."

Beginning with his move to supportive living in his early forties, Jimmy took meds for type II diabetes, cholesterol, depression, and an enlarged prostate. He used eye drops and ear drops. He took over-the-counter meds for constipation, allergies, and hemorrhoids.

"I don't feel right. I just don't feel right, Joyce." Whenever he invoked my name, I knew he was serious.

"How long have you felt this way, Jimmy?"

"A few years."

My heart sank. Why had he been feeling so low for so long and not told me? Why hadn't I recognized the signs and done something sooner? I went into driver mode again, got a list of Jimmy's medications and researched them. I learned that Jimmy was being prescribed the new expensive designer drugs often. He was in a chemical straitjacket with the latest anti-depressant.

"My brother is not a contributing member of society since he's been on this drug," I said to the doctor. "He doesn't call his family anymore. He stopped going bowling with his friends. He's having trouble at his part-time job and not following his supervisor's direction. He's not shaving and showering every day. His color is pale, he sweats profusely, his jaw clenches, he's lethargic, and he sleeps all the time. What other options are available?"

"Let's put him on Prozac. It's an older drug but it's the granddaddy of anti-depressants and is proven," said the psychiatrist.

I'd known people who benefitted from this drug and others who didn't, but agreed to give it a try.

"First, we have to wean him off the Latuda and get him to baseline," said the doctor. "I want to see what he's like without any drugs."

Jimmy gladly weaned off his latest prescription but his baseline proved intolerable. He became belligerent, yelling profanities, and eating excessively. He kept shouting, "I want to die!"

Within sixty days of beginning the Prozac, Jimmy was smiling, staying well-groomed and showing behavioral improvements. However, in another three months, there came more verbal outbursts. He was disrespectful, profane, and argumentative with the social workers. He'd disappear in the middle of the night and talk about hurting himself.

Each time a call came from the social worker, I'd pull out my "Jimmy file" and record what she reported. My notebook turned into a binder that grew large quickly. It included notes from important conversations I had with Jimmy, too. Then I'd call Lynne or Alison to tell them the latest episode. I regretted interrupting them at work so kept the news brief and typically asked one to notify the other of the latest development. They'd sigh first, then ask questions or make suggestions I hadn't considered. We'd confer on what to do next. For example, we got him off allergy meds and prescription toothpaste (he'd had a dental implant) that he no longer needed and had cost too much.

I felt a little better sharing the load with Lynne and Alison. Then, and many times since, I silently thanked my parents for giving me two sisters. No matter where we've been in our lives or what we may have going on in our own families, we've always been united in doing what's best for Jimmy. I imagine it must be lonely and difficult being the sole sibling of a needy brother or sister.

As much as I tried to hide the stress of managing Jimmy's episodes from my daughters, I'm certain it showed in my quiet and sometimes reclusive behavior. It took concerted effort to listen to their stories about school and friends with the ever-present soundtrack of Jimmy playing in the back of my mind. While I kept many details from them, they knew to allow me space to decompress. I'd usually retreat to my bedroom with a book. My daughters have always shown compassion and understanding of my role as their Uncle Jimmy's sister.

Whenever my husband asked about a day that involved me acting as Jimmy's advocate, I'd sigh. After a while, repeating the story became tedious and only aggravated my stress level so I stopped. He, too, knew to simply give me quiet time. Sometimes I wanted to cry or scream "Why me?" but I never felt the right to do so and generally acquiesced with a groan. After all, Jimmy had a difficult life. Unwilling to admit, at the time, my life had been difficult, too.

7

Despite my love for Jimmy, I often wished for freedom from responsibility. However, when it slowly happened during childhood, I felt a void and didn't know how to fill it. Even though his early childhood patterning had ended on Stoneybrook Lane, the pediatrician said we still needed to do certain exercises to help my brother develop. The exercises were aimed at making him more coordinated and getting him to respond better to his environment. In the fifth grade we moved to Penn Avenue, a slightly larger single-family stone house a half-mile away from our old home. By that time, neither Jimmy nor I wanted to do the exercises. We wanted to be upstairs watching TV with the rest of the family. Nevertheless, every night, for about a year, we'd slowly click our way down the stairs for a half-hour routine in the basement.

On the left side of the stairs, Dad installed white wall paneling and a dropped ceiling. He raised the floor and laid red rubber floor tiles that continued up the stairs. When he finished, you could still see some nail heads under random squares. Each step had a silver, ridged metal strip nailed across the edge, so you couldn't descend the stairs without hearing the click, click, click of metal against your shoe. The bottom stair was a half step that startled everyone when they stepped

Our Penn Avenue house, Drexel Hill, Pennsylvania

off it the first time. Kids thought it was cool and did a little dance on the bottom step—up and down, up and down.

Jimmy and I put our entire bodies on the floor, belly side down like a couple of turtles, and began with the creeping exercise. An old couch and a Singer sewing machine that collapsed into its own cabinet surrounded us, as did every stray household object or bag of nonessential items my mother couldn't bear to throw away. We didn't like creeping because our faces came too close to the cold floor. Sometimes we'd get stuck, unable to find a matching rhythm. It reminded me of the soldiers on the TV show *Combat* that Dad watched.

After the initial creeping exercise was out of the way, Jimmy and I moved on to the crawling exercise. We morphed from turtles into cats, moving around in circles on our hands and knees, slowly and deliberately. We preferred crawling to creeping because we could control the movement of our bodies more easily and see each other better.

Next were Jimmy's eye exercises. Jimmy would sit cross-legged on the floor while I took the shade off a small lamp, exposing its light bulb twelve to eighteen inches from his face. I moved the lamp slowly to Jimmy's left, center, right, and back to center. I continued this pattern for a minute or two, with breaks in between. He had to keep his head still and move only his eyes to match the direction of the beam of light. Continued exercise would strengthen his eye muscles and improve his peripheral vision.

I felt conflicted doing the exercises with Jimmy. In some ways, I resented the time I needed to spend with him. I knew my mother and father had many obligations managing our family and home, but I don't remember Lynne or Alison doing exercises with Jimmy. Lynne's role as first-born was "Mommy's helper." As the baby, Alison got off easy. Dad said by the time Alison came along, he was tired and let things go with her. I always figured because Jimmy and I were closest in age it made sense for me to partner with him. It was my role and I accepted it. I liked the quiet activity. I felt certain no girl my age could relate to how my brother and I spent time together.

Sometimes I'd see people pointing or laughing at Jimmy when we were out shopping with Mom. I felt embarrassed and wanted to physically distance myself from my family. The other part of me wanted to punch the jerks and tell them to stop staring. Jimmy never seemed embarrassed by anything. If he tripped or knocked over a display in the grocery store or dropped his fork in the diner, he'd just go with the flow. He might have uttered "Oh" or "Darn it!" or "Sorry." Otherwise he couldn't have cared less who watched or what anyone thought or said about him.

Sometimes I wished I could be oblivious like him. He'd let things go while I intensely examined and dwelled on situations.

I was always on alert when out in public with Jimmy–on alert for people making fun of him and, by extension, me. I thought no other family had issues to deal with the way my family had with Jimmy.

On the other hand, being Jimmy's sister made me feel important and grown up. It reassured me to know I had the recognition and trust of my parents in ways neither Lynne nor Alison did. Always eager to act mature, the role of Jimmy's keeper came naturally to me since it's all I knew.

Jimmy's willingness to be patient and cooperate with the exercises amazed me. If anything, I was the one who itched to get done so I could read or lounge on my bed and listen to the radio. I felt sorry for my brother who had to go through those repetitive, exhausting exercises. I didn't like them either, but it was worse for Jimmy because they were harder for him to do. Plus, he was getting bigger and bumped into things often.

Jimmy never got antsy nor did he get mad at me during our exercise time together. If he disagreed or needed a rest, he'd stop without protest. When that happened, I rested with him on the floor. He liked the one-on-one attention. He performed better when one person focused on him rather than being in a room full of distractions or too many people. We'd complete as many of the other exercises as we could.

"I'm tired, Joyce," he'd say on occasion.

"A few more, Jimmy."

"But I'm tired."

I couldn't prod Jimmy any further. I remember the ambivalent feelings of wanting to complete my assignment honestly and please my mother, and wanting to please Jimmy, too.

"Okay, but we can't go up now. Mom will know we didn't

finish. Let's sit here for a few more minutes and then we'll go upstairs," I decided. As a child, thirty minutes feels like hours when you're not doing something fun.

"Did you do your exercises?" Mom would ask when we joined the rest of the family in the living room. Jimmy would follow my lead. We'd nod in tacit agreement, never divulging our secret.

Eventually, the prescribed exercises stopped because Jimmy's adolescent body was developing and getting stronger. He started receiving other services through the school's special education department. His vision improved so he didn't need to wear glasses anymore. Jimmy began to show more independence. He didn't need me as much anymore. That became clear the day he almost gouged my eye out.

One December when we were in our early teens, Jimmy opened a Christmas gift Mom and Dad's friends bought for the family—a game of darts. Although definitely not a game my parents would buy, in a gesture of appreciation, Dad hung the dartboard on the wall of the finished side of the basement. Some of the neighborhood kids were playing down there over the holiday break. I stood in the doorway watching the activity and tried to remain invisible. I didn't know how to play darts nor did I care to. All I knew how to do down there was sew a straight line on the green Singer sewing machine and practice Jimmy's exercises.

I watched the boys elbowing each other, shouting and having a great time. In fact, I felt left out and jealous of Jimmy having friends at the house to play. They were hooting and hollering around the table hockey game and taking turns with the darts. I crossed the room and before I knew it, a dart whizzed by me, missing my face by mere inches. I instinctively put my hands to my head and gave Jimmy a scared and questioning look. He was old enough to know better. Dad had warned us all about the dangers of using the darts.

"You're in my way, Joyce!" Jimmy shouted, trying to act like the boss in front of his friends.

To this day, I wonder if he threw that dart on purpose or if it was an accident. Either way, he knew he'd made a mistake as soon as it happened. Yet, I still felt like an extra body in the room and actually blamed myself for being in his way. There was an implicit understanding in the family that we should do anything to make Jimmy happy. If that meant raucous play down in the basement, then so be it. If it meant only one child could host friends at the house, then it would be Jimmy's friends.

The boys stopped for an instant when they heard Jimmy yell at me. I looked around the room in defeat. No one came to my aid. Without obvious injury or blood, they simply returned to playing table hockey, Matchbox cars, and darts.

Trembling, I slowly made my way upstairs.

"What's the matter, Joyce?" asked Dad.

"Jimmy threw a dart at my face," I tattled, secretly hoping he'd get in trouble.

Dad jumped up from his seat in front of the TV.

"What? Are you all right?" he asked bending down to get a closer look at me.

"Yeah," I said, feigning a dramatic pose with palm to cheek. "It almost hit my eye."

"Damn game. I knew I shouldn't have hung it up," he said on his way out of the living room.

I followed Dad down the basement. Part of me wanted to see Jimmy get yelled at and the other part was afraid of Dad's anger. His scowl scared me and his physical strength could be intimidating.

The ruckus abated when Dad pounded down the steps. Jimmy's friends stood frozen in mid-play but Jimmy had mysteriously disappeared.

"Jimmy? Jimmy! Where are you?" yelled Dad as he rushed back and forth from the finished to the unfinished side.

My imposing father stomped to the unfinished side of the basement and paused in front of the hot water heater. The newly minted dart-thrower had vanished. Dad instinctively opened the small closet door under the stairs where we hung out-of-season clothes. There he found Jimmy, squashed between the coats, palms facing out at his shoulders in surrender.

"I didn't did it. I didn't did it," Jimmy said nervously.

Dad grabbed Jimmy's shirt and pulled him out of the cramped closet.

"Did you throw a dart at Joyce?"

"I didn't did it! I didn't did it, Dad!"

"You could have hurt Joyce, do you know that?" Dad released his grip while Jimmy's shoulders remained crunched up to his ears. Dad was never too hard on Jimmy, no matter what his son did, accidentally or on purpose.

That signaled the end of the dart game. Dad marched to the finished side of the basement as the kids scurried to the corner of the room to get out of his way. He yanked the dartboard off the wall, collected all the darts, clicked his way upstairs, barged out the back door and threw the infelicitous Christmas gift in the trashcan.

I felt out of place in the basement and avoided my parents in the living room. On my way upstairs I stopped mid-step to eavesdrop on Dad and Mom.

"That Jimmy," Dad chuckled again after mimicking Jimmy's unique response: "I didn't did it. I didn't did it."

"Is that what he said?" my mother laughed with pride.

Never mind that Jimmy could have blinded me, Dad and Mom celebrated their son's newfound ability to assert and defend himself. I felt incidental to the scene.

My feet froze midway on the steps. Why were they laughing when I could have lost an eye? I continued up the stairs and flopped onto my bed.

I didn't know where I fit in. Jimmy had found a group of friends to play with but I didn't. I didn't know how to be recreational. Homework gave me an excuse not to play. Books became my friends. They provided me comfort and I liked the solitude and quiet that reading afforded me. Otherwise, my time was spent with endless responsibility for Jimmy and household chores in our meticulous home. Put the clothes away, pass the vacuum, set the table, dust the bottoms of the dining room chairs, wash the plants, sweep the kitchen floor. I never felt like I had the freedom to play.

It was clear Jimmy and I were growing apart. It didn't seem long ago that we first moved to Penn Avenue and spent time in the basement doing exercises when I was in charge.

"I didn't did it" became a favorite family refrain.

8

When Jimmy engaged in more activities with his friends, I had more time to pursue my own interests. My older cousins, whom I always looked up to, played the piano and I wanted to play as well as they did. So in the fourth grade I began piano lessons.

My first teacher, Miss Fallon, was a gray-haired woman in the neighborhood. She led me through a primer set of books. After the lesson, I'd walk to my Aunt Tootsie's house a few blocks away to practice at the white baby grand in her living room. A few months later my parents bought a Baldwin piano. As the centerpiece of our modest home, the cherry wood spinet looked beautiful. It looked rather than sounded beautiful because I was inconsistent with piano lessons in my youth.

A few months into lessons with Miss Fallon, my parents invited friends over and they asked me to play.

"Joyce has potential," said family friend Mr. Kornblatt when I finished. "I think you should enroll her at the Drexel Hill Conservatory of Music." My parents respected his opinion particularly because he was a school principal as well as a pianist.

So I auditioned for the conservatory owner—a rotund man with a duck walk and thinning hair.

"Very good," he said after I'd completed a favorite piece.

"Now I'm going to tap some patterns with my hand on the piano here and I want you to listen carefully and repeat each pattern."

When I completed each quick pattern exactly, he complimented me. I was astonished and thought: *Well, maybe I do have talent.*

I felt worthy and important attending a conservatory. The music of Beethoven, Mozart, Chopin, and other composers seemed instantly familiar to me, as if it emerged from my subconscious and flowed from my fingertips onto the piano keys. I loved the sound of classical music but hated practicing, especially the dreaded scales. The director told my parents I had all the talent but not enough desire. At some point during my apathetic teen years, the lessons stopped. I preferred listening to pop music like Carole King's *Tapestry*, Billy Joel, James Taylor, and Carly Simon.

Then one day, Mom surprised me by saying she bought tickets to see the famous pianist Arthur Rubinstein in Philadelphia. Only three tickets: one for Dad, one for her, and one for me. I was stunned. Not only would I witness a world-class musician perform at the historic Academy of Music on Broad Street, but I'd have private time with Mom and Dad. No siblings in my way. That had never happened before.

Dad wore a suit and Mom and I wore Sunday dresses for the occasion. There was a happy buzz in the car as we drove into town. When we walked into the music hall, my jaw dropped. I'd never seen such opulence. The chandeliers, murals, columns and gilded architecture astounded me. Mom bought me a souvenir program and we made our way to the red velvet seats where she and Dad sat on either side of me. We clapped when the aging pianist with white wavy hair dressed in a tuxedo slowly made his way to the gleaming ebony grand at center stage. He flipped his tuxedo tails behind him before sitting on the piano bench. He commanded the concert hall while tapping his gnarled fingers up and down the keyboard. The classical music stirred me.

I asked for lessons again. Mr. Messina came recommended by a family friend. Tall and slightly hunched, he lumbered into our living room dressed in a suit and tie and carrying a worn leather briefcase. He had one cloudy eye. I found it difficult to look at him. He'd sit to my right and out of the corner of my eye I could see him moving his whole face to the left as I played so he could see with his good right eye. I couldn't concentrate on the notes. I was aware of my family listening and waiting patiently in the kitchen. My entire body constricted on the piano bench. I felt sorry for Mr. Messina and feared him at the same time. He would get angry when I made a mistake or didn't comprehend something new.

"No, no, no!" he'd bang his fist on the piano and startle me. "The Sabre Dance must be quicker!"

I tried. I even got through the first few pages of Moonlight Sonata. Then one too many times he put his hand on my hip, pulling me on the bench to reach the top of the scales, closer to his seat. I finally told Mom and that was the end of Mr. Messina.

So I dabbled with favorite sonatas and waltzes on my own, playing them over and over again, enjoying my solitude. It gave me freedom from chores around the house. I had a talent no one else in my family had and I didn't have to explain it to them. The piano music gave me a mental escape.

Still, I felt guilty about using the living room to play while Dad sat patiently waiting to watch TV. If someone walked into the living room, I panicked. I feared making mistakes. I wanted to hear myself play dramatic, classical music without all the practicing. But I didn't want it badly enough because the feet of the piano bench didn't make any new indentations in the carpet for a few years.

After graduating college, I'd go to a friend's house and swoon over her mother's effortless piano playing.

"Why don't you take lessons again?" suggested Mrs. Beston. "Go to the Bryn Mawr Conservatory of Music. It's down the road from Villanova."

"I don't think I'm good enough to study there."

"Sure you are."

With Mrs. Beston's encouragement, I auditioned at the conservatory in the elegant Main Line mansion dating from the 1870s. Again, I felt important there but surely out of place, surely not good enough. To my surprise, they admitted me. This time I felt motivated and paid for the lessons myself.

My instructor was a gentle, bearded guy in his late twenties. He'd been a finalist in the Van Cliburn International Piano Competition. We started off slowly. After a couple of months, I'd delay the start of my lesson by chatting him up. In retrospect, he must have detected my lack of passion. He was too easy on me and we both knew it.

Then a substitute teacher surprised me one week. She had no time for small talk and showed no mercy. However, I remember thinking as I descended the stairs after my lesson how she really challenged me. Even though she intimidated me, she was precisely the type of teacher I needed.

Despite that, I didn't ask to switch teachers. I longed to summon the passion I witnessed in the faces of other students, but it wasn't there. So I left the conservatory.

In my late twenties, I had a conversation with my parents on the beach one summer day about my regret.

"Why didn't you push me?" I asked. "You should have forced me to practice every day."

"We couldn't push you," said my father. "You had to want to play for yourself."

"What do you mean?"

"It had to come from within, not from your mother and me."

The piano relocated with me to my apartments and homes for twenty-six years. When my parents visited, Mom would ask with a trace of hope, "Ever tickle the ivories, Joyce?" Or Dad would tap a few keys himself while I listened from the kitchen with pangs of guilt and remorse. The piano was a constant reminder of my failure and the money Mom and Dad wasted on me.

I lugged around an old dream long after I'd outgrown it. Finally, Dad suggested selling it and replacing it with a desk and I did. It took me years to figure out I was more suited to music appreciation than music performance. The piano paved the way to my love of fine arts. Dealing with the complications of adult life and caring for Jimmy, I continue to find refuge in museums, observing the art and architecture in great cities, buying handcrafted gifts, watching any kind of dance, listening to the Boston Pops orchestra, and of course, reading.

9

My father could manage dozens of men on a dangerous construction site for forty hours a week but was challenged leading a Boy Scout troop of seventeen disabled boys for a single hour every Sunday afternoon.

As a foreman, Dad supervised a brotherhood of union ironworkers. He trained the guys how to read blueprints, estimated labor time, ordered materials, assigned tasks, and recorded hours worked and days absent. On job sites of bridges and high-rises, Dad gave direction once—loudly. Worker safety was his paramount concern. We knew whenever an accident occurred on the job or when Dad had to lay someone off because he became very quiet at home.

The crew knew their jobs and put in overtime if necessary to get the work done and provide for their families. Laughs and pranks with Babe diverted them from the numbing cold of winter and the sweltering heat of summer.

Everyone called my dad by his nickname, Babe. He hated his given name, Amleto, and anguished over the misfortune of inheriting the name of his father, an Italian immigrant. Dad got annoyed writing Amleto, spelling it, saying it, and explaining it. He thought his older brother should have been sacked with the dubious moniker. Instead, Alfred had the distinction of being named after a dying family member who, as it turned out, didn't die when expected shortly after Alfred's birth. Then, when my grandmother called her second son "the babe," the name stuck. Dad preferred his nickname to Amleto and delighted when people would ask, "As in Babe Ruth?"

My father was a sociable guy. He participated in games of basketball, volleyball, and tennis, and enjoyed watching a tough competition, too. However, initiating a club did not exactly fit his personality type. For one, it meant finding energy for a group of developmentally disabled kids every Sunday night after a week of backbreaking labor and a weekend of home improvement projects.

One of Jimmy's teachers suggested a Boy Scout troop for kids like my brother. My parents liked the idea and attended a meeting in the teacher's classroom to establish the group. As Dad described the family tale, all except one father stared at his shoelaces when Dad asked who'd be willing to co-lead the troop. He was relieved when Frank Littlefield finally raised his hand. Now all Dad had to do was find a meeting space.

"Father," he said to the priest at St. Bernadette's rectory, "I'm going to lead a Boy Scout troop for my son and his classmates. They all have special needs and we think it will be a beneficial program. We need a place to meet. Can we use one of the classrooms or the church basement for an hour on Sunday nights?"

"Mr. Poggi, is it?" the priest replied mispronouncing the name with a hard 'g'.

"Poggi," Dad corrected.

"I'm sorry, but I can't allow that."

"Can't allow it?"

"No," he answered with a bowed head.

"Father," said Dad, searching for eye contact, "twelve of the boys in the troop are members of St. Bernadette's parish."

"I'm sorry, but I can't open the school or church for a group of handicapped boys."

After the first holy communion incident, I was surprised Dad went back to St. Bernadette's to ask for help. I suspect he still held out hope for belonging at the church, both for Jimmy and the family as a whole. When rejected again, Dad sought a welcoming hand elsewhere.

"Here's the key to the church, Mr. Poggi. Take whatever you need," said Reverend Goodheart of the Collenbrook United Church. The pastor waved his hand around indicating Dad should make himself at home in the Protestant church, where my father had never before set foot. Dad stared at the pastor speechless, astonished by the stranger's generosity and trust.

One Sunday evening, the scouts were horsing around the church hall when there was a loud crash. One of the Callahan twins broke the wooden lectern used for Reverend Goodheart's sermons. Exasperated, Dad had to apologize to the pastor and expected to pay for the repair. Worse, he feared losing the space for the scout meetings and having to search for a new location.

"Reverend, I'm very sorry but the boys broke your lectern." Before Dad could suggest repayment terms, the Reverend Goodheart deflected the situation.

"They're kids," he said, untroubled, with another wave of his hand. Again, Dad was left nonplussed by the Protestant minister's forgiveness and simple words of kindness.

One year, Dad and Mr. Littlefield took the boys on a weekend camping trip to French Creek. The last time Dad had slept in a tent was more than twenty years prior when stationed in the Philippines and Japan during World War II. Upon dropping their sons and camping gear off at the Protestant church that Friday night, the parents sped away, abandoning Dad and Frank to manage the camping adventure by themselves.

Dad concerned himself more with the boys' safety than with showing them an outdoor adventure. On the drive to the campsite, Dad heard whiny, pleading voices:

"Mr. Poggi, when are we going to get there?"

"Mr. Poggi, can this car go any faster?"

"Are you lost, Mr. Poggi?"

"I think you're lost, Mr. Poggi."

During the course of the weekend, the whining persisted.

"Mr. Poggi, when are we going to eat?"

"Mr. Poggi, I have to go to the bathroom." Dad heard snap, snap, snap from a camper's sleeping bag.

Danny was small and frail, afflicted with cerebral palsy. His mother gave Dad a handful of Danny's medications along with specific instructions on how and when to dispense the pills. Dad noticed the kid didn't have much equilibrium when they saluted the flag at the beginning of the trip. *Thump!* Dad turned and saw Danny on the ground. Startled, Dad rushed to administer aid, unsure what kind of emergency he'd be facing, only to hear the young scout say, "I'm okay, Mr. Poggi. I fall all the time."

Dad wondered if the weekend would ever end. His patience had been tested to its breaking point.

"How could I get angry at those boys?" he asked reflectively. I wondered how he could relax and have a good time. Clearly, it was work for him.

Dad set up camp and helped them with their sleeping bags. He built a campfire, prepared meals, and kept them entertained, all the while keeping count of the scouts to be sure no one got lost or injured, and repeatedly checking his watch.

Finally, on Sunday night, Dad waited in the darkened parking lot of the church for several parents to pick up their sons. When that didn't happen, he ordered the remaining malodorous scouts into his station wagon with their gear, and drove the boys home himself.

"I was so wound up," said Dad, "I gripped the steering wheel so tightly, I thought it would bend."

Dad reported the camping trip to the Boy Scout council and casually described how the weekend ended with him playing chauffeur.

"Oh, you can't do that, Mr. Poggi. That's against the by-laws," said the council representative.

"What do you mean, against the by-laws? Why can't I drive them?" he asked.

"You have to have extra insurance to transport the scouts in your personal car," said the rep.

"I'm already insured."

"Well, if you continue to drive the boys in your car, you'll need to have at least one hundred thousand dollars worth of insurance."

"What?" my father screamed in disbelief. "That's ridiculous. Is the council going to pay for the insurance?"

"Oh, no! We don't have that kind of money. You'll have to buy the additional insurance yourself."

"Well, then, I hereby resign as leader of this Boy Scout troop."

"Yo, Ro. Five years is enough," Dad told Mom afterwards. "I'm exhausted. Let someone else do the work." They agreed Jimmy had a fun experience and received the camaraderie he needed. Even Jimmy let Dad know he was getting bored with the troop. Finally, Dad could relax on Sundays, knowing he'd be back to work Monday morning managing only one boys club.

I always viewed Dad as an impatient man. He huffed while waiting in line at V&B deli, swerved in and out of highway lanes shouting "dumb ass." He constantly hurried us along in our chores, clapping his hands and saying, "C'mon, let's get done!"

Dad's loyalty to our family was obvious: daily bear hugs to Mom and his kids; commitment to his job, always out of the house before the sun came up and rarely missing a day of work; tinkering around the house, and his willingness to drive us anywhere and buy us whatever we needed. It wasn't until he was in his eighties and told me this Boy Scout story one rainy afternoon when I realized the reservoir of patience Dad summoned to lead the troop, and the unheralded commitment he made to Jimmy and his fellow scouts.

The neighborhood boys became Jimmy's real circle of friends. He got plenty of outdoor exercise playing basketball and street hockey with them. He lost weight (the jelly belly rolls where I used to blow raspberries on his stomach to make him laugh were gone). They'd appoint him goalie, which he loved since Bernie Parent, the popular goalie for the Philadelphia Flyers, was his idol. Bigger than the other kids, Jimmy knew how to stop a puck. He loved wearing the cumbersome goalie pads and sports gear with his orange and black Flyers shirt, even though he could barely move when entering the house through the back door, blocking the sunlight. With his goofy grin and the volume of his voice turned up a few notches, sweating and red-cheeked, huffing and puffing, he'd tell us how many saves he made that day. I envied his ability to fit in and play. He moved effortlessly among the boys, able to relax and enjoy friends.

Alison had an easy-going nature, too. She was always the spark of fun in our family. Everyone got a big kick out of her. She kept busy usually riding her bike with a new friend or getting invited to someone's house for dinner. She'd come home winded and smiling, often with her pants or shirt torn indicating a carefree afternoon of fun on the monkey bars at the playground. Lynne had all the privileges of being the firstborn. She hung around with Christine and they both worked at a restaurant and told tales about eating ice cream in the walk-in freezer. She cruised around town with her high school sorority sisters. She had a boyfriend and always seemed to be whispering to her friends, making it clear that I was not "old enough" to know whatever it was they discussed.

I didn't have that ease to hang out with girls and never felt I could invite them over to the house. I had a friend named Carolyn who lived two doors up. She attended St. Bernadette's and had a lot of responsibility, too. She had to babysit her little sister frequently while her mom worked. When she finished the list of chores her mother set out for her, she'd call me and I'd go to her house to eat cookies and fudge (her mom kept a well-stocked kitchen full of snacks). We'd polish our nails and watch the soap opera *General Hospital*. Other than that, I didn't have a sense of play. Rather, I only remember chores and responsibility.

It's no wonder that in adulthood I prioritized cleaning the house before going out to do something recreational. I'd be at work during the week and thoughts about the upcoming weekend went to laundry and cooking and other chores instead of planning a bike trip or a hike. I tried to stay in the moment at the playground with my children or at a *Disney on Ice* show, knowing time with them was fleeting. Yet even on days at the beach or on ski slopes with my husband and daughters, my mind raced with the housekeeping to-do list that had to get done when I returned home.

10

Twice a year for spring and fall cleaning, Mom grabbed the rooftop with both hands and shook the house out the way she shook the dining room tablecloth out the front door after a holiday dinner. Mom dusted and vacuumed every day—sometimes twice. She could often be seen with a rag in her hand, wiping surfaces: tables, counters, appliances, doors, windows, venetian blinds. Despite this, spring and fall cleaning meant "deep cleaning" as she called it.

Every April, Mom would attack the closets for a week while we were in school. Even when I phoned her thirty years later and asked what she was doing, she'd answer, "Cleaning out a closet." By the weekend, the trash barrels out back burst with bags of frayed bath towels, outdated over-the-counter medicine, broken toys, stained or torn clothes, and beat-up shoes. The closets became super-neat again with the hangers all going in the same direction, shoes lined up, and new bath towels neatly folded in perfectly aligned stacks.

One spring Saturday morning, I was jarred awake by the blaring sounds of John Philip Sousa's marching band playing on our stereo. I groaned knowing what it meant.

"Wake up!" Dad yelled from the bottom of the stairs.

Although Dad's cheerful voice indicated a good mood,

I knew a day of chores lay ahead with Mom giving lots of directions. I was convinced other girls my age played while I worked. However they amused themselves, I was certain it didn't involve a dust rag.

By the time we got out of bed, Dad and Mom had already tackled the first-floor windows, cleaning and raising the storm windows and installing the brush-scrubbed screens, and were ready to reach the second floor. Dad would position himself on a wooden ladder outside facing Mom inside with Windex in one hand and paper towels in the other.

"Babe, you missed a spot," she'd tap-tap-tap on the window with the nail of her pointer finger.

Once the windows were squeaky clean, Mom scoured every inch of the three bedrooms, ceiling to floor. I awaited my instructions knowing Mom had a detailed plan of action for the day.

"Joyce, empty this bucket of dirty water in the toilet and refill it with Pine Sol and hot water from the tub," she said.

"Here, Mom," I said, returning with the pail.

"Okay, now take this rag, dunk it in the bucket, then wring it out and wipe down all the baseboards."

I didn't know why I was chosen to get on my knees for that job when Alison was smaller.

"Joyce, you're as slow as molasses," she said, tapping her foot while holding the vacuum extension in her hand. "C'mon, let's get done!"

What was molasses anyway? She used that phrase with me a lot, like when she'd send me to get her cigarettes or the encyclopedia. It hurt my feelings when she said I was slow as molasses even though I didn't know what it meant. I don't recall her using the phrase with Jimmy or my sisters. The first time she told me I was slow as molasses, I thought she said "slow as my ass is" and I was shocked. Then I thought it might be a curse word. I knew by the tone of her voice that slow as molasses wasn't a compliment and didn't ask her the definition. She'd probably have given me her pat response: "Look it up in the dictionary."

My older sister Lynne (who, like Mom, moves as fast as lightning) and I cleared the knick-knacks off the bureaus and wiped them down, stripped the beds and climbed up and down the stairs with laundry loads and bags of trash. Dad moved the furniture including lifting the mattresses and box springs so Mom could vacuum the inside corner lip of the metal bed frame with the long attachment.

"See?" she said, pointing proudly to the dirt being sucked up. Who knew we'd find dust there? We'd Windex, Pledge, wipe every horizontal and vertical surface, re-shelve the books and piggy banks, make the beds with fresh linens, and finally vacuum the rug. And it wasn't even noon.

While the four of us cleaned inside, Jimmy and Alison were assigned the garage.

"Jimmy, you and Alison go outside and try to clean the garage," Mom would say.

"Okay, what should we do?" he'd ask.

"Take the bikes and everything out and make it neat."

Since Dad never parked the car there, the garage served as a storage shed for the bikes, lawn mower, tools, beach chairs, and assorted dusty or rusted items. I don't know what the two of them did out there but it never amounted to much. I think they just moved junk around because it didn't look any cleaner or more organized at the end of the day than in the beginning. They certainly didn't work at the break-neck speed Mom set for

Lynne and me indoors.

Mom's vague instruction didn't really matter. She couldn't tolerate two more people in her way during all her deep cleaning. Besides, Jimmy could be clumsy (another word Mom disliked). He often tripped and tended to knock over tabletop items. And since he'd grown bigger, Mom wouldn't take a chance of him tripping over a bucket of Pine Sol or the vacuum cleaner cord.

It didn't take Alison long to make a beeline for the back door. As far as I can remember, she never passed the Hoover, dried the dishes, or put away the clothes. Alison played. She had lots of friends and tons of energy. I was jealous of her freedom. Mom and Dad found their baby amusing and cute. I didn't.

"Remember the time you were lost, Alison, and we found you down by the pharmacy perched on top of the mailbox eating Sugar Babies?" Mom would laugh.

"How about the time we were on Martha's Vineyard waiting for the ferry and couldn't find her?" said Dad. "She waved from the upper deck of the boat while the rest of us were stuck among all the other vacationers trying to board," he chuckled.

"Oh Alison, you're so funny," Mom would say while Lynne and I cleared the dishes. That's because Alison parked herself in the desirable seat near the wall between Mom and Dad where she couldn't get out without forcing them to move their chairs.

Around noontime, we'd all sit down at the kitchen table for a lunch break. Dad would unpack cold cuts, fresh rolls, and Tastykakes from V&B, the local deli. It was a great reprieve before the dreaded downstairs cleaning. We were only half done and already exhausted. Not Mom. Like the Energizer bunny, she kept going and going. And no one could rest until she did.

"Wash and dry the plastic fruit . . . and the ceramic bowl," said Mom. "Then when you're done with that, I want you to dust the bottom of the dining room chairs."

"Okay, then will I be done?"

"No. You still have the plants to do. I'll be in the basement doing the laundry," she said, carrying an armful of bedspreads and curtains. "I'll tell you when we're done."

That spring, I decided I'd had enough. We had finished lunch and I stood at the kitchen counter wiping the leaves ("Front and back, Joyce.") of all the houseplants (artificial and real) with a wet paper towel. I felt trapped and was fed up with the never-ending house cleaning.

I imagined other girls my age having fun styling each other's hair, trying on each other's clothes, flipping through the pages of *Tiger Beat*. If I heard Mom say, "Joyce do this" or "Joyce do that" one more time I was going to scream. I needed space. So I slipped out the back door and walked away.

I walked up Penn Avenue and turned left on Cedar Lane, a shady cross street which runs parallel to the main street in town. With each block, I glanced over my shoulder to see if Mom or Dad were driving up to rescue me. Nope. Surely someone from our neighborhood would stop me soon and ask where I was going.

My stroll was unexpectedly peaceful that balmy day. I felt liberated in a strange way. No one bumped into me. No one asked me to fetch something. My hands were empty. Gone were the familiar, annoying noises of my household: the low drone of the vacuum cleaner, slamming doors, pounding feet, and family voices yelling for me to get something, bring something, carry something, do something. The scented air of spring in bloom propelled me forward even though I didn't have a destination in mind.

About an hour later I arrived at the Aronimink Elementary School, a pretty stone building with a playground bigger than my school, Drexel Hill Elementary. I checked a few doors and discovered the school locked and the playground empty that Saturday afternoon. I meandered around the building and crouched down in an alcove. I hid in a way to make myself partly visible to the main cross street in case sirens started to blare. For a half hour, I waited there, hugging knees to chin. It was an effective hideaway, not too difficult for someone to find me—if they were searching.

As I sat waiting, I wondered how a search might affect Mom's spring cleaning schedule. Would she dare leave the vacuum cleaner in the middle of the floor with the cord loose? Or would she finish all the housework before looking for me? It was a tough call because Mom liked routine.

I imagined a massive town search would be under way. Lost ten-year-old girl, brown hair, brown eyes, four and a half feet tall, eighty pounds, wearing shorts, t-shirt and Keds sneakers. I'd be the focus of everyone's attention and loved the idea of people talking about me and wringing their hands with worry and admiration.

Mom and Dad would be frenzied, maybe even teary-eyed. First they would search the neighborhood. They'd get Lynne to help, and our neighbors, Mr. Verdi and maybe Mr. Cavalli, would help, too. They'd search two blocks in each direction and comb the elementary school playground and the junior high school nearby. They'd check the cemetery where kids often wandered. Maybe they'd call Aunt Tootsie to see if I walked to her house six blocks away. If all this failed, they'd call the police and file a missing person report. When they found me, there'd be a tearful reunion of hugs and kisses. Police cars would block traffic, their flashing red and blue lights visible for many blocks. I'd be in the center of it all. Maybe a television crew would show up and I'd be on the six o'clock news.

I figured Mom had about another two or three hours of housework before she started wrapping things up. I felt certain I'd been gone for as long as that, maybe more. It started getting chilly in the alcove. I realized if I wasn't rescued, I'd still have to walk all the way home. Thinking it might take an hour, I started back. Pretty soon I'd have to pee. My mouth was dry and I wanted a soda. I wondered what Mom would cook for dinner. There was still a chance of a dramatic rescue on my return trip down Cedar Lane.

I walked back, alone with my thoughts. No car or bike stopped for me. No one recognized me. The return home seemed longer. Finally, I turned onto Penn Avenue and ambled into our driveway. The garage door was open. It was still a mess in there. The bicycle built for two, beach chairs, and other stuff were strewn in the driveway and neither Jimmy nor Alison were anywhere in sight.

I opened the back door with some hesitation and stepped into the kitchen, careful to close the door latch without making a sound. The house was still, the windows sparkled, and the smell of lemons permeated every room. I tiptoed through the dining room and living room leaving footprints in the vacuumed carpet. Upstairs in my room, the blue area rugs and bedspreads were fluffed and perfectly aligned.

For a moment, I thought everyone was out searching for me or at the police station. When I realized they never would have left the doors unlocked, my private glee turned to disappointment. I went back downstairs anticipating a reunion. Would they hug and kiss me or yell at me? Would they ask where I'd been?

Nothing. When Mom emerged from the basement carrying a basket of folded clothes, she didn't even ask where I'd been. She acted as if she'd just seen me five minutes earlier. I waited for some reaction. There was none. She just sighed after her arduous day of housework and said, "I feel like the wreck of the Hesperus."

Maybe she thought I was cleaning the garage with Alison and Jimmy all this time. Out of the corner of my eye, I searched her face for signs of worry or concern, but she never skipped a beat—continuing her housekeeping. No knit brows or sad face. Same for Dad.

Could they have been playing a trick on me, pretending they didn't know I was gone? Maybe they assumed I was off doing something useful, since I was, after all, a dutiful daughter. Maybe they figured I went to my friend Carolyn's house. It depressed me to think of myself as forgettable.

Crushed, I spent the night tossing and turning. Ultimately, I decided not to bother telling anyone about running away. Nobody cared anyway. My job was to be good, clean the house, and help Jimmy. Why bother pulling another stunt like that? In the end, all it got me was cold, thirsty, and alone again. It certainly didn't get me any attention I may have been seeking.

A few days later, I asked Mom, "Was I a mistake?"

"No. You were a pleasant surprise," she answered. "God made sure you were easy to take care of." She went on to explain that because she had her hands full with Lynne and Jimmy before I was born, God blessed her with a "mild child" as her friend labeled me. Then Alison, our little whirlwind, came along four years later.

I became tired of being stuck in the middle and not even squarely in the middle. As the third of four children, I wanted a definitive label like my siblings: Lynne the oldest, Alison the baby, and Jimmy the only boy. In our black Dodge Dart, Alison won the coveted seat up front between Mom and Dad. I got sandwiched between Jimmy and Lynne who had window seats. My feet straddled the hump.

I tried to stay out of the way. Eventually, I adjusted to the lack of attention and liked feeling invisible. If I could have blended into the wallpaper, I would have. Often I'd walk around the house on tiptoe, trying to go about my day as unobtrusively as possible. I didn't want to burden Mom and Dad with any trouble. If I did my homework and chores and followed the rules, I'd be fine. Jimmy needed attention, not me. As he grew up, his needs became less physical and more emotional.

I continued to ask Mom if I was a mistake and her answer was always the same. On one occasion when I was in high school, she continued the conversation.

"Actually, the only child who was planned was Jimmy," she said. "Isn't that ironic?"

I never summoned the courage to ask her to elaborate. In my late teens, I began to wonder if God sent me to help Mom and Dad with Jimmy.

"You know," she mused years later when my career was thriving, "if Jimmy had been born normal, he'd have been the smartest of all my children."

At the time, I was struck and didn't know what to make of her statement. Moreover, I felt slighted that she verbalized it to her studious daughter. Was I supposed to make up for Jimmy's shortcomings? Did I surprise her by achieving the success I had worked so hard for? Despite my curiosity and emotional wound, I never raised the topic again because I didn't want to debate my mother and possibly hurt her feelings. I learned over the years to simply nod or say "Uh-huh."

Things began to crystallize for me when I became pregnant at age thirty-three. I reflected on my impending role of mother and examined my own family dynamics. After the jubilation of finding out I was pregnant, fear set in. Like most women, I worried about my baby's health and began questioning family history. Did I carry a gene that might cause my child to be intellectually disabled like Jimmy? I couldn't ask my mother about her medical history because she always cried when talking about Jimmy's birth.

She recounted various theories about her second pregnancy. She bled in the first trimester. During one prenatal appointment, the doctor told her he thought he heard two heartbeats and asked if twins ran in the family.

"Yes," she replied. "My mother-in-law was a twin."

"It's too soon to tell. I want you to go to Miseracordia Hospital for an X-ray."

Dutifully, she complied.

When I think of this, I imagine baby Jimmy calmly and warmly gestating in my youthful mother's womb before jolts of electromagnetic radiation pierced his forming skull, damaging a tender, developing brain.

My father cursed that doctor his entire life, insisting those X-rays scrambled Jimmy's brain. Mom was never sure. She insisted the cord wrapped around Jimmy's neck cut off oxygen despite the doctor's claims that the delivery was uneventful. In the 1950s, women were knocked out during labor while fathers paced in the waiting room. Was it the X-rays, lack of oxygen, or the early bleeding that could have been Jimmy's twin that caused Jimmy's disability? My parents would never know the origin of the detour of their lives.

Raising the topic with Mom when Jimmy was age thirty-four was not something I wanted to do. My parents were in a different phase of their lives by then. Jimmy's neighborhood friends moved on and his sisters were newly married. I felt alone again, unable to discuss my pregnancy fears with Mom.

I researched mental retardation and considered going to Boston hospitals for genetic counseling but didn't follow through. It would have required getting details from Mom and I wasn't up for the emotional toll it would take on her or me. I'd take my chances and pray for a healthy baby.

Sixteen weeks into my pregnancy, I returned to my parents' house for Christmas.

"You look adorable," said Mom, with her hands still on my shoulders after hugging me.

"Thanks, Mom. Do I look pregnant?"

She dropped her jaw, put her palms on her chest and instinctively fell back a few steps. This would be her first grandchild. When she phoned her friend minutes later with the happy news, I overheard her from the kitchen say, "Not Alison. Joyce!"

As the career woman, apparently I never projected maternal ambition. In my youth, I didn't play with dolls or have a favorite stuffed animal. I never had a babysitting job or talked excitedly about having babies the way my college friends did. It wouldn't occur to me why until years later. All my maternal instincts had been directed toward Jimmy during my childhood.

11

Even in the sixth grade at age ten, my teacher identified the caregiver in me. I'd finally received recognition and was elected Safety Guard of the Month. At the time, I had no clue why. In retrospect, I must have projected maturity and responsibility to my peers, always being such a quiet goody two-shoes. Instead of wearing the girls' round, metal badge strapped to my upper arm, that month I had to wear a red boys' style red badge (all the boys wore a white badge) that crossed the chest on a diagonal and wrapped around the waist. I rolled the badge up and held it while on duty.

"Why aren't you wearing your special badge?" asked Miss Laughlin from her desk one day after the school day ended.

"It will wrinkle my dress," I answered from the doorway, not wanting to disappoint her.

"Aren't you proud of the recognition?"

"Yes, but Miss Laughlin, this is a boys' badge."

"Nevertheless," she said, tapping a pencil, "you should wear it proudly instead of swinging it by your side like that."

It wasn't exactly the way I wanted to stand out. I liked being recognized as a leader among my classmates, but would have preferred reading the morning announcements aloud instead of having to wear an ugly red strap across my chest.

Some kids made fun of Miss Laughlin because she was fat, but I liked her a lot. She had wavy, black hair. Her hair cream made it look greasy because I never saw a loose strand. She had rosy cheeks, a double chin, and a pointy nose. When Miss Laughlin laughed, her chin disappeared into her neck, reminding me of Grandmom's pasta dough. When Miss Laughlin rose from her seat, her left hand grasped the back of the oak chair and she flattened her right hand on the desk to push off. Every time she did that, I wanted to groan "*un-n-nh*" for her. She favored a solid blue dress that fit snugly around her belly and wide rear end. When she shuffled to the blackboard, she picked her dress away from her chest with her thumb and forefinger then tugged it down at the hips. When she returned to her desk, she'd put both hands on top for a secure landing. Once seated, she'd fan herself with papers, sometimes two-handed. As a preteen, I didn't know about menopause.

"Open the windows, Joyce," she'd say. Never mind that it was January and everyone else in the classroom wore sweaters and wool clothing. I'd lean over the radiator, grab the two metal handles at the base of the enormous windows facing State Road and hope they glided up on the heavy roping inside the sash on the first try.

For the first four months of the school year, Miss Laughlin seated me in the first row directly in front of her desk, second seat, behind Dennis Garapetian. A funny, chubby kid, Dennis had olive skin and dark brown hair he moved away from his eyes with a swift jerk of his head. His short attention span meant he regularly pivoted in his seat to pester me.

"Turn around!" I'd whisper loudly. He'd grin trying to get a reaction from me. I'd nudge his shoulder, trying not to laugh. "I mean it. Turn around!" Thirty seconds later, his clown face would block my view of the blackboard, and again he'd knock a pencil out of the groove of my maple desk. "Cut it out, Dennis!" I'd say, bending down to pick it up.

Dennis would lift the tabletop portion of his desk and say "Pssst," before shooting a spitball through a straw at his buddy in the next row.

"Shh!" I'd say, trying to pay attention to Miss Laughlin. Dennis constantly asked me for paper or a pencil. I'd sigh and dip into my supply, hoping he'd stop bothering me.

One day, Miss Laughlin noticed my frustration while she pursed her lips to suck on hard candy again. I was fairly certain she had a stash in her top drawer with her Ticonderoga pencils and red Bic pens.

"You can hit him, Joyce," she said matter-of-factly between sucks. "It's okay. You have my permission. Go ahead and hit him if you want."

I wasn't sure I heard her correctly. Was she telling me to break the rules? If I did, I knew it would be sinful, too, and then I'd have to go to confession. Nobody in my family hit. I could never hit Dennis, or anyone for that matter.

Dennis froze in his seat, only his head moving from Miss Laughlin's concaved cheeks to my stunned face. He must have wondered if I would really hit him. It dawned on me years later that Miss Laughlin wanted me to do what she wanted to do: hit Dennis to get him to shut up and behave.

Partway through the year, Miss Laughlin decided to move my seat and position me directly behind the new boy in class, Tim O'Donnell. Tim had transferred from St. Andrew's School. Rumor had it he got kicked out. I took my new seat (the second seat, again). By now I understood Miss Laughlin expected me to rub off on this restless, freckle-faced, red-haired kid and somehow calm him down. I disliked sitting in the middle row of the classroom. It made me feel exposed and Tim's constant fidgeting distracted me. I yearned for my old seat by the window even if it was behind unruly Dennis.

Unfortunately for me and luckily for Miss Laughlin, I showed more patience with Dennis and Tim than she did. Her recognition felt good but I wished she'd have assigned me more interesting projects like the ones she gave Susie Gillen, the teacher's pet. Perky Susie was super-smart, smiled without her gums showing, sang like a nightingale, and scored the lead in the school play. Miss Laughlin singled out Susie to distribute papers, decorate the bulletin board and, best of all, read the weekly announcements on the P.A. system from the principal's office.

I showed up every single day, on time, and sat quietly. I suppose that's why Miss Laughlin counted on me for other jobs. She commended me on my neat handwriting and assigned me to write the names of all her students, alphabetically, on the manila attendance sheet every month. She gave me the job of clapping the erasers on the granite steps outside after school, probably because she didn't want to huff and puff her way up and down four flights of stairs. All of Miss Laughlin's assignments made me feel important but I didn't understand why she kept giving me housekeeping and babysitting jobs instead of fun jobs like stapling notices on the bulletin board. Just once I would have liked to read the school announcements on the P.A. system. That would have been fun and engaging but I didn't possess the outgoing personality and ready smile of the kids who were repeatedly chosen to do that job. I got the boring jobs of cleaning the erasers and washing the boards. Apparently, Miss Laughlin deemed those tasks better suited to an introvert like me.

When the school bell rang at three o'clock I only had to cross the street and walk the length of three houses to get home. Although I couldn't wait to be back in the classroom learning again, I didn't miss Dennis or Tim. Helping Jimmy came easily to me compared to the challenge of dealing with Miss Laughlin's troublemakers.

Jimmy was only a year older than Dennis and Tim. Unlike them, Jimmy had no difficulty sitting still. With his left hand, Jimmy wrote in large block letters in his composition book. For his math homework, he worked very hard to line up the numbers so he could add them together. He listened when I gave instructions and he never talked back. Sometimes his mind wandered as his gaze drifted away from me. It had always been difficult to determine what he was thinking or if he was thinking at all.

At least my brother didn't behave like Dennis and Tim. My parents instilled discipline and good manners. They maintained an immaculate home and car, paid bills on time, and modeled a strong work ethic. They taught us responsibility at an early age beginning with making our beds and saying grace before meals.

Sometimes it took Jimmy a while, and my family and I may have had to repeat ourselves, but eventually he always did as he was told. He'd put away his hockey gear or clean up the cookie crumbs and milk droplets he left on the kitchen table.

I often waited for Jimmy to find words to express himself. I waited for him to print the words in his composition book and listened to him read aloud, sometimes syllable by syllable. My instinct was to speak the words for him so that he wouldn't stumble and we'd get done faster. However, I knew that by jumping in I wasn't helping him, only reducing my personal wait time. I implicitly knew Jimmy's learning time was more important than my free time.

He used his pointer finger under each word when we were at the kitchen table. He'd sit motionless, usually slack-jawed, while I repeated a lesson to him. Then he'd say, "Oh, I get it. I get it now. Yeah. Yeah. Yeah, yeah, yeah." We'd break into a big grin every time he had a eureka moment. When I saw Jimmy relax, I relaxed. I was proud of both of us.

Although being with Jimmy forced me to be patient, there were plenty of times growing up when I felt exasperated waiting for him: to keep pace with me on the way to school, to put on his coat or tie his shoelaces, to finish his math homework so I could read or watch TV.

I used to wonder if his thoughts were organized, if he made mental lists like I did. I wondered if he searched for words before saying them or if he'd develop a wider vocabulary. In my late teens, I wondered how much unused storage his brain had—if it exceeded whatever portion of his brain was damaged. I wondered if he'd remember tomorrow what I taught him today. I wondered what went on behind those big brown eyes of his. I still wonder.

I'd be a college graduate before realizing all the life lessons Jimmy taught me. Even though in my adulthood I've been guilty of rushing others to speak and have huffed and puffed while waiting to be served at a restaurant or store, those early lessons with Jimmy forced me to develop patience and compassion for others.

In my forties, I used to shop at a supermarket that employed a middle-aged man with cognitive impairment who reminded me of Jimmy. They both collected carts in the parking lot. I'd let the eager guy push my cart and unload grocery bags, then chat a few minutes before giving him a big tip. I knew that's what Jimmy would have wanted.

My mother used to say with hope in her voice, "Maybe if I'm nice to another special person like Jimmy, then someone out there will be nice to my son." I've never forgotten her wish and try to extend kindness, even if it's just a smile, to others in need of compassion from a stranger.

12

Ever since I received the call from the social worker and learned Jimmy had threatened to jump off a balcony, I've asked myself why I hadn't been able to detect the depth of his sadness. Was it the distance, or did I subconsciously wish to avoid rather than confront him? Was it easier to let his social workers deal with the matter so I could direct my mental energy elsewhere?

I anguished at home alone while Jimmy received psychiatric treatment in the hospital. He hadn't expressed himself much after Mom died and, since we lived hundreds of miles apart, I couldn't observe his moods or behaviors. Still I felt culpable. My line of thought led to another person I had known, De. Like Jimmy, he had suffered quietly without my knowledge.

My mother rarely called me at work, so on a late March morning in 1995 I suspected someone was sick. Her voice sounded different, calmer. Like a sad song, she said, "Joyce . . . De died" with emphasis on De's name.

De was my first love, if that's what you call it at age nine. His real name was DeForrest, after his father, a prominent ob/gyn doctor. When a teacher would roll call the first time, De blushed explaining his name. He corrected people when they called him Dean and he crossed out the second "e" when they wrote his name like a girl's.

We met in the fourth grade when I transferred to Drexel Hill Elementary. De had shiny, straight brown hair like mine and I considered it the key reason we made a cute couple. I figured if we married and had children, they could be models for Breck shampoo ads on the back cover of *Family Circle* magazine. De looked trendy wearing blue jeans cuffed at the bottom. He'd get in line behind me on the playground when the teacher blew the whistle to indicate recess ended. I could feel the heat of his body without him ever touching me. He might brush my arm in the hallway when we returned from art or music class. It was the closest I'd ever been to a boy, other than my brother, and I liked the new, tingling sensation when De came near me.

In the cafeteria I'd slide my tray along the counter with my five-cent carton of milk and occasional block of butterscotch swirl ice cream, searching for De. He ate lunch at the same table every day with his crowd. He always sat in the corner seat facing my table of friends. We'd manage to lock eyes a few times before darting them back to our trays. After lunch, he kicked a soccer ball on the field with the boys while I played four square with the girls. For three years De and I glanced at each other with uneven smiles.

When the school bell rang at three o'clock, sometimes he'd walk me home. I don't remember what De and I talked about on those afternoons but we chatted more comfortably in the privacy of my yard than on the playground. Something about De's quiet and often serious demeanor made me want to be near him. When that happened, I felt breathless.

Although I yearned for De to kiss me, I refused to climb over the stone wall of the cemetery across the street and sit among tombstones with the fast kids playing Spin the Bottle. De never asked me to, but I had a hunch he would have played the game if I did. By the end of sixth grade, I wondered if De would still be interested in me when we entered junior high.

In the spring of 1969, before moving up to the junior high school, all the sixth-graders were swapping autograph books, a present from our teachers. The first entry in my dark red book with flowers on the cover was from De. He wrote a verse: "Roses are red, violets are blue, sugar is sweet, and so are you."

Later that day, De asked for my book, insisting he wanted to write something else inside. A few moments later he returned it then scurried away without saying a word. I broke from the crowd on the playground, peeked inside the book and read what he added under his poem: "I still like you. I like you more than anyone else does. Please don't drop me. I like you much too much."

Heat rose to my cheeks as I quickly closed the book before anyone could notice. De liked me a lot, maybe even more than I liked him. He recorded his intimate feelings about me. What did it mean? Where would our relationship go? It wasn't only shy glances anymore. I tucked away my autograph book and resolved not to ask anyone else to sign it. No one except me would witness De's permanent expression of love.

Despite hopes from friends for a blooming romance, our preteen love fizzled during those apathetic early 1970s. He was into soccer and I developed a crush on someone else.

Then early in my sophomore year of college, I was pleasantly surprised to see De on campus. He had a careful, deliberate gait that crisp September day and approached me with a winsome smile. Handsome in his clean, dark blue jeans fitting perfectly over his tall thin frame, he held a stack of books against his hip. His shiny brown hair, soulful brown eyes, perfect teeth, and clean skin hinted of my first desire for him years earlier. Those features appeared more refined now. Soft-spoken, he explained how he decided to transfer to Villanova and was a commuter like me.

We didn't share any classes but bumped into each other on campus now and then. Although our preteen love never rekindled, we remained friendly the next three years. Occasionally, he would offer me a ride to or from school in his silver Volkswagen Scirocco. One night at the end of our senior year during finals week, De drove me home from the college library where we had been studying.

"Thanks, De," I said as we approached my house, reaching for the car door handle. He startled me when he put his right hand on my left arm.

"Will you stay here with me a while?" he somberly asked.

"Uh, okay. Sure." I felt vulnerable and wondered if he wanted to kiss me.

He turned off the ignition, then reached in his shirt pocket, lit up a joint and offered it to me.

"No, thanks," I said waving my hand at the smoke. I feared my mother detecting the odor on my clothes.

On the half-hour ride home that moonlit night in early May, conversation had been easy. But sitting in the parked car, a melancholy wave washed over him. Was he worried about final exams? Where to go after graduation? Neither of us had firm plans.

"What's up, De?"

He shook his head then took another hit. I waited a moment before persisting.

"De, tell me. What's going on?"

Still no words.

"Come inside," I said.

"No, I can't."

"Why not?"

He stared out the windshield. An invisible shell closed around him.

"Come on, De," I said, nudging his shoulder, trying to cheer him. "Come inside and I'll make you a meatball sandwich."

"No," he answered softly. "Stay here with me a little while longer, okay?"

We sat in silence a few minutes more until he finished the joint.

"Are you okay? You're going home now, right?" I pleaded, trying to make eye contact with him.

"Yeah, I'm fine," he said, avoiding my eyes.

"Good night. Thanks for the ride, De."

I paused before gathering my books, then hesitantly stepped out of the car. I closed the door gently and rested my hand on the door handle another moment. Then I bent down and looked at him through the window with a weak smile. Maybe he gave me one last shy smile or maybe he stared out the windshield. I don't remember.

That was the last time I saw De.

When my mother finished reading me the obituary from the *Philadelphia Inquirer*, I was still in shock. No cause of death was listed. De died at age thirty-seven. My jaw remained slack and a rainstorm gathered in the corners of my eyes. In slow motion I hung up the phone, my sweaty palm momentarily stuck to the receiver. My shoulders shook as I dropped my head over my arms on the desk and sobbed.

The awkward images of our youth flashed before me. There stood De, an adorable, shy fourth-grader, head bowed, hands stuffed into the front pockets of his jeans, kicking pebbles between us in the schoolyard while trying to figure out what to say to me. Approaching my front porch. Pleading with me to let him write something else in my autograph book. In his high school soccer uniform. As the handsome, lanky, smart, introspective guy slipping between the socializing crowds on the campus green. And finally, in the car that night.

De graduated medical school and brought hundreds of lives into the world as an admired ob/gyn doctor in Atlanta, where no one knew his father's name. He never married or found someone special to create his own family. The note said he couldn't live with the pain any longer.

I wish I had put my arms around him that last night.

I hope I wrote something equally tender in his autograph book.

Remembering De's death, occurring nearly eighteen years prior to Jimmy's hospitalization, made me realize that I had to be more attentive to my brother's behaviors and moods. After Jimmy would get discharged from the hospital, I'd make greater efforts to call him more frequently. I'd encourage him to pursue new hobbies, make friends, and socialize. I hoped my attempts to help restore him to better mental health would work.

13

The nurturing role always suited me. After all, I'd been assigned it as early as age five during Jimmy's patterning days. Maternal figures surrounded me: aunts, other mothers in the neighborhood, babysitters, older cousins, and teachers. These women were gentle, caring, smart, and well dressed. Whether managing a large family, a home, or a classroom full of unruly students, they portrayed confidence, outer beauty, and inner strength. As a result, I aspired to be like them.

By the time I put away the elementary school autograph book in the summer after sixth grade, I immersed myself in all things feminine to prepare for junior high. Finally, my hair had grown out and no longer would I have to suffer the embarrassment of getting it cut at the barbershop.

The first time I went to the men's shop, I sat with Alison along a wall of mirrors. I remember thinking the barbers were effeminate because of the way their pinky fingers stuck out, clipping and snipping. I searched for girl magazines or puzzle books on the low tables but only found sports and car publications.

Mom guided Jimmy to the red vinyl barber chair and told Bob the barber to give her son a burr—the popular boy's cut. By then, Jimmy had lost all his blonde hair from his toddler years. It turned dark brown like mine. When the second barber finished shaving the neck of an old man and turned toward Alison and me, Mom caught my eye.

"Okay, Joyce, your turn."

"Me?" I asked. Was she kidding? That was for boys! Up until this point, Mom snipped our hair at home.

"Yes, honey. The barber will give you a cute pixie haircut," said Mom, reaching her hand to guide me.

Why couldn't I keep my shoulder-length hair like Lynne and her friends? Mom used to twist strands of my hair with bobby pins in two rows of pin curls every night and then wrap my head in a hair net. I loved those bouncy curls the following morning. They made me feel like Shirley Temple.

I wanted to glue myself to the seat, but had to obey Mom. Slowly I stepped to the barber chair while the cheerful man with slicked-back hair grinned at me. I wanted to disappear, embarrassed to be in third grade and, once again, next to Jimmy. Twin boys should have been getting haircuts together, not brother and sister. My face flushed fire engine red to match the vinyl barber chair. I could barely look at myself in the mirror.

I wanted to go to a beauty parlor. Mom went to a ladies' salon across the street, so why couldn't she take Alison and me there? I wanted to be with women who sat under hair dryers that resembled plastic helmets while they flipped through *Life* and *Look* magazines, kicking their crossed legs. I always dreamed about having my hair rolled in curlers. At the time, I thought only adult women were allowed in a salon. If that was the case, then where were girls like me supposed to get their hair cut? It simply wasn't fair to smell shaving cream instead of ladies' hair spray.

I glanced through the storefront window to see if anyone I knew might be watching. The barber snapped me back to attention as he flapped the lightweight polyester apron to his side before placing it widely around the large chair and fastening it at the back of my neck. He tapped my shoulders then rubbed his hands together as if he were about to begin a piano concerto.

To avoid my reflection in the mirror, I took inventory of the hair supplies on the counter in front of me. A tall, round container resembling blue dish detergent sat in the corner with a silver metal lid. Inside it, several black combs disinfected. Shaving cream, razors, and a wooden shaving brush standing on end with its soft beige bristles splayed upright. No bobby pins, no barrettes, ponytail holders, or hair bands. No fashion magazines or girl hairbrushes, no hair spray—not a speck of anything feminine. I didn't belong there. How was I supposed to look feminine if I got my hair lopped off at the barbershop?

I closed my eyes and dreamed I was at Grandmom's mahogany vanity table using her hairbrush with the soft bristles. I wanted long hair covering my back like Lynne's and Christine's. Then I could clip tortoise-shell barrettes behind my ears. Even better, I could pull my hair back in a high ponytail with a ribbon and swing it back and forth to flap against my ears.

Instead, I felt cold water being sprayed over my head. It didn't take the barber long to present me with a short, blunt cut exposing my ears and neck. He combed my straight, dark brown hair from the whorl at the crown of my head to the front and down the sides, without a part. He acted proud to have cut a little girl's hair for a change the way he stood back and tilted his head this way and that examining my head. Then it was Alison's turn for her pixie cut.

On Monday morning, I decided to wear a hat to school because I was embarrassed and ashamed of looking like a boy. The long stocking cap with a brown and white zigzag pattern had a yarn tassel at the pointy end. It grazed my waist and made me feel like I had long hair. All day kids asked me why I didn't remove the hat. I told them I wore it to keep warm and then changed the subject.

After six hours of wearing the wool on my head, I couldn't keep up the charade. Once safely out of view of classmates on the playground, I pulled the stocking cap off my hot head on my walk home. Fresh air hit my short, messy locks and sweaty scalp. I tried to calculate how long it would take me to grow out my hair and how to tell Mom I didn't want to go to the barbershop anymore.

That experience reinforced my desire to seek all things feminine in my teen years. It affected me so much that, ever since, I've kept my hair shoulder length. Furthermore, when my daughters were young, I kept their hair long enough for ponytails.

Once I became a mother, I realized Mom took all three of us to the barbershop simply because it was quicker and cheaper. Still, those visits were embarrassing. Bad enough I was lumped with Jimmy at school, Catechism, and home and still I had to be treated like a boy and get a haircut with him at the barbershop?

At my grandmother's house, I'd gaze into her vanity mirror and realize that even when my hair grew out, I'd still be stuck with a narrow, sad face. My brown eyes were set too closely together, like Jimmy's and Dad's.

My eye teeth resembled fangs. I could have landed a child's role on *Dark Shadows*. Too much gum showed above my teeth when I smiled so I'd cover my mouth with my hands. My upper lip thinned and exposed the ridges of pink covering my teeth. I had the appearance of a chimpanzee, and my big brown eyes and straight brown hair didn't help with the image. I'd practice smiling in front of the bathroom mirror, trying not to let my gums show. As many times as I tried, it simply did not work. If I laughed or smiled spontaneously, there was no way I could consciously force my lips to cover the gummy ridges. If I smiled slowly, then I had time to spread my upper lip over the gums, but then it looked fake. To this day, I rarely smile broadly for a photo.

I inherited my gummy smile and high palate from Dad. Jimmy's mouth was the same except he never had a gummy smile. His two front teeth protruded a little, but he didn't have buck teeth. Our dentist recommended an orthodontist for both of us. Before we got braces, Jimmy and I each had two teeth pulled. The dental surgeon yanked the premolars behind each of my canines to make room for those fangs to descend and line up with the rest of my teeth.

Once a month on Saturday mornings, for a year or two, Jimmy and I would go to the orthodontist's office. Sometimes Lynne drove us there. She'd get a big kick out of flashing her Pepsodent smile to all the self-conscious kids in the waiting room with racks of metal in their mouths. The only thing the orthodontist ever did was tighten the metal strip across both our front teeth. Jimmy wore elastics to align his jaw, though. It grossed me out whenever he removed the elastics at the dinner table and put them between his plate and mine. I'd cover them with a napkin.

The doctor's big thumbnail repulsed me. It was long, thick and curved up like a yellow claw. I recoiled whenever it touched my mouth or skin as if it were a diseased talon. I couldn't figure out why a grown man would keep a disgusting thumbnail like that, particularly a man who made a living by putting his hands in people's mouths.

Neither Jimmy nor I got a whole set of tracks on our teeth like I had hoped. I'd learn years later that my parents had only so much money to put toward orthodontia because it wasn't covered by Dad's insurance. So Jimmy and I wore our retainers infrequently. My bottom teeth grew out a tad crooked but not so bad as to make me want to cover them. Anyway, when I smiled, they didn't show. My fangs finally grew into place but there was nothing the orthodontist or anyone else could do about my gummy smile.

Since there was nothing I could do to change the anatomy of my mouth, I became fastidious about my teeth, brushing and flossing two, three, or four times a day. I didn't want them to yellow. I didn't want them to wear thin like the underside of Mom's front right tooth. Over the years, her tooth had become partly translucent from using it to separate the bobby pin to put her hair in a French twist and my hair in pin curls in my early elementary school days.

Even though my younger sister Alison's teeth were straight, I definitely didn't want to spend countless hours in the dentist chair like she did. She had so many cavities filled from all the saltwater taffy, Sugar Babies, and Charleston Chews she ate. She still loves candy. She alone probably financed her dentist's vacation home with the hours she logged in his chair.

When Jimmy was in his late teens, he used to grind his teeth at night loudly enough to wake me up and make me fear an intruder. However, his high school portrait with a big bow tie and smile of straight teeth turned out fine.

My high school photo, on the other hand, was a disaster.

All gums. I begged Mom to order the photo of me with a softer smile.

"No," she said pointing to the one with the full gummy smile. "This one looks more like you."

"But Mom, I look ugly in that picture! It will be in my high school yearbook for everyone to see forever."

"Oh, stop. You look adorable. That's the one I'm ordering."

Growing up, I had asked Mom several times for a vanity but she said it wouldn't fit in the room I shared with Lynne and Alison. The master bedroom we occupied was already crowded with three beds, three desks, two dressers, and a nightstand.

Whenever we visited my grandmother, I would sneak into her bedroom before dinner and sit at her vanity. I'd pretend to use her Coty dusting powder and examine my brown eyes and wonder if there was a chance they might still turn blue. I longed to be pretty and feminine like my older cousins and Lynne and her friends but didn't know how that would happen, especially when I sported the pixie hairdo.

I couldn't imagine Grandmom preening over herself. She wore floral housedresses and occasional lipstick. To me, she focused on cooking and keeping a spotless home more than anything. She'd be hunched over behind the rectangular, white-speckled, Formica table with grooved chrome trim on the side, making ravioli. Flour coated the table, her hands, and the full-sized print apron that draped over her sagging bosom. She'd pause to accept the kiss I planted on her loose-skinned cheek then return to her pasta. She spooned a ricotta cheese dollop onto every square, dabbed it with her pointer finger, and then covered the squares with another thin layer of her homemade dough. Grandmom cut the dough into individual squares with a knife, then dipped a fork in egg wash and pressed it around all four sides of the ravioli to secure them closed.

A stainless steel bowl turned upside down on the table meant she had another batch to make. Grandmom lifted the bowl and peeled a perfectly smooth ball of dough from the tabletop with her wrinkly hands. She let me touch the powdery softness and I dusted the flour from my fingertips. When she kneaded the dough, the skin under her upper arms flapped back and forth, appearing doughy too. Then Grandmom grabbed the wooden rolling pin while I watched in amazement at her magic.

My family ate in Grandmom's dining room decorated with doilies and lace curtains. I felt like an honored guest eating from a linen tablecloth because every other day of the week my family ate at our kitchen table with plastic floral placemats. Grandmom stood at the head of the table and ladled ravioli, meatballs, and sausage for each family member.

"Joyce, pass this to your brother and hand me your plate, honey," she'd say. She may as well have poured her heart onto the plate because this was pure Italian love from nostril to belly. I'd have loved to replicate the aroma and feeling of family unity in Grandmom's dining room with my children, but we lived 350 miles from my parents. Although I still made Italian dinners every Sunday and regaled my daughters with stories about my family history, I regret that they missed out on the benefits of regularly seeing their grandparents and experiencing that unique relationship more deeply.

∼

My siblings and me with our maternal grandparents
Philadelphia, Pennsylvania
1966

Before bringing fork to pasta, I soaked in the magical sight and inhaled the aroma of tomatoes, garlic, and basil. Swirls of steam rose to my nose. Then I took a piece of fresh Italian bread and dipped the crusty slice into the gravy, alternating between bites of ravioli. A soft explosion of ricotta in my mouth was followed by Grandmom's gravy bathing my throat in warm delight. One night, I remembered round-bellied Grandpop addressing my mother while nodding his head toward me and saying "*Questa–lei sta mangiando tutto!*" This one, she's eating everything!

Afterward, I'd help bring the dinner plates into the kitchen to make room for dessert.

"Look, Jimmy," Grandmom would say walking in from the kitchen. "Coconut custard pie. Your favorite!"

"Ooh. Coconut custard pie! For me?"

It was the same routine every time, yet everyone acted surprised. Grandmom usually offered a tray of pignoli cookies (Mom's favorite), bought from Termini Brothers bakery, along with her homemade pizzelles.

After dessert, I'd often play cards with Jimmy on the gray wooden floor of Grandmom's porch. Jimmy loved playing cards just like Grandmom. She gave him a new deck now and then. He wouldn't let anyone hold the cards. He slowly slid them out of the blue box and kept the deck straight, his pointer finger poking out all the while he stacked the cards evenly. Then he shuffled and shuffled and shuffled.

"C'mon Jimmy!" I said. "That's enough shuffling. Let's play!"

"Uh-kay. One more shuffle." I think he liked to show off his manual dexterity.

He dealt each card slowly and laid it on the porch floor with a snap. Then we began a game of war. Sometimes we got mixed up with the face cards and I'd run into the kitchen where Grandmom stood with a dish towel over her shoulder washing the plates in a tiny white ceramic sink. She paused, her hands still in the sudsy water when I showed her the two cards Jimmy and I insisted were winners. "Queen beats the jack," she said softly.

"Thank you, Grandmom," I said, skipping back out to the porch.

"Ha-ha, Jimmy. I beat you." Even though it didn't happen often, Jimmy hated to lose. He might say, "Oh darn it!" or "I should have won." Sometimes he said nothing and, instead, jutted out his lips like a fish mouth, shuffled the deck, and dealt again.

"Let's play Go Fish," he said. He preferred Go Fish or

Rummy because they were less about luck. He remembered who picked up which card and he usually won because of his sharp memory. He loved to lay his cards down with multiple snaps, give his goofy smile, and a "ha-ha-ha" belly laugh when surprising any of us with a winning move.

When it was time to leave, Grandmom waved her hand indicating we should follow her back into the dining room. The floors squeaked when she took slow steps in her sensible shoes that bulged with bunions. The soft jingle from her wrist came from the bracelet with the names of each of her ten grandchildren inscribed on a gold charm. Jimmy's charm read James, named after Grandpop. Grandmom opened the top left drawer of her mahogany sideboard and gave each grandchild a quarter, along with a kiss goodbye. I wiped her wet kiss from my cheek on the way out through the vestibule hoping she didn't see.

A few years later on a sunny day at the pool in June of 1970, at age twelve, I returned from the vending machines with a package of Kent cigarettes for Mom. Instead of eagerly waiting for me, she was picking the towels off the cyclone fence and stuffing them into the canvas tote bag without folding them.

"Quick," she said. We're leaving." My mom's sister had called the pool office and tracked us down.

Grandmom had been sick with emphysema and in and out of the hospital for a few years. I wasn't old enough to visit her there. I knew she took a lot of medicine evidenced by the pill bottles lining the kitchen window ledge behind her when she made ravioli. Although I remember her wheezing, she never really appeared sick to me.

Mom told me that Grandmom stepped out to her porch in West Philadelphia, sat in her wicker rocking chair, and tilted her head back. She must have needed a rest from all the cooking, cleaning, and laundry. She asked Grandpop to get her a glass of water and when he returned to the porch, she was dead. Heart attack.

During her funeral, I sat in a fog. I didn't cry and thought it callous and wrong but Mom and Dad said it was okay not to cry. Jimmy followed my cues when to sit, kneel, and stand. I kept my hands folded in prayer and would elbow him as a reminder to do the same.

"Mom," I whispered, leaning in front of Jimmy, "What's that awful smell?"

"Shh." She leaned toward me and said, "That's called incense. It's used for funerals."

Sitting in the pew next to Jimmy and Lynne, I watched in amazement at the pallbearers carrying Grandmom's casket down the aisle on their shoulders only, their hands clasped in front of them below their waists. I still couldn't believe my grandmother's body lay in that casket and decided then and there my dead body wouldn't lie in a casket when I died. It creeped me out to think about being buried underground.

I thought about Grandmom and how her house on Marlyn Road wouldn't be the same. It wouldn't smell like an Italian dinner. The floor wouldn't creak under the weight of her footsteps. She wouldn't sit at her vanity and use her dusting powder, comb, or hairbrush. No more hugs or wet kisses. The woman who taught me how to make a bed and fold the corners tightly, who I'd seen flour pasta dough but never powder her nose, was dead.

I find it comforting to know my grandmother died the way she lived—in a thoughtful and inconspicuous way. On a summer day, on the porch, in her rocking chair.

Twelve years later when I was preparing to move into my own apartment, Mom surprised me.

"Look what I found for you at a yard sale!" she said, pointing to the dusty piece of furniture in the driveway. "You can take it to your new apartment."

I hesitated. "Thanks, Mom. But . . . it's so old and dirty."

"Are you kidding? This is a gorgeous piece. All it needs is a little elbow grease. When we clean it up, strip it, and stain it, it'll look brand new. You'll see."

"Really?"

"Yes," she said stepping back to get a broader view of her find. "Honey," she said putting her arm around me, "I know you always wanted a vanity but we couldn't fit another piece of furniture in the bedroom with you and your sisters. Now is your time."

Even though I've used the vanity for years, like my mother and grandmother, I never wore much make-up or spent hours in front of a mirror. Despite always being dress-ready, the role of caregiver superseded self-indulgence. We spent more time tending to the house and family than on personal beauty treatments. Inner strength was more important. My grandmother needed strong resolve to get through the Depression and other straining economic times. My mother needed it to advocate for Jimmy. Looking back, that inner strength took root in me at a young age and developed. I would draw on it in my career when I found myself as the sole female manager in conference rooms full of men whose opinions may have differed from mine. More so, I'd draw on it when faced with challenges related to Jimmy's care and well-being.

14

Growing up, I thought I was supposed to be an unobtrusive, mature, good girl. Other kids ran unabashedly on the playground, charged down the streets on bikes, laughed easily, had a great sense of wonder when playing games, and said, "Let's go!" I wished I could do that, but being playful didn't come naturally to me.

Mom recognized my pursuit of femininity and eagerness to grow up even though I was still a preteen. She took me to Weinberg's department store to shop for a first-day-of-school dress before entering junior high. It's one of the few times I can remember going someplace alone with her. She spotted a pretty green and white dress with an empire waist and puckered sleeves and told me to go into the dressing room to try it on. As we left the store, I skipped across the parking lot swinging the distinctive pink and gray striped bag with Weinberg's written across it in bold script.

While older teenagers rocked at Woodstock that summer, I eagerly waited for Paul the mailman to deliver an important envelope. On the last day of sixth grade, Miss Laughlin had promised a letter from the junior high school would be mailed home indicating the assigned section and homeroom for all seventh graders. In late August, an envelope with the school's return address arrived. I bounced on tiptoes while Mom took her time opening the letter.

"You've been assigned to section 7-11," she said.

Seven eleven. I liked the rhyming sound and would enjoy writing 7-11 on homework assignments and test papers.

"You have to report to homeroom 116 on the first day of school," she continued.

I could barely wait to get out of my summer shorts and wear my first-day-of-school dress and new shoes. I wanted to go shopping at Bond's for school supplies immediately.

In the same stack of mail was another letter with details for Jimmy, one grade above me. Absorbed in my own excitement, I forgot about him going to the same school. For the past three years, he'd been bused to other elementary schools with special ed programs while I attended Drexel Hill Elementary. We already knew Jimmy would be assigned to the special education classroom.

"What's Jimmy's homeroom number?" I asked Mom.

"Jimmy is assigned to room 116, too," she said.

"He's in the same homeroom?" I said as she continued reading the letter.

My smile disappeared as she nodded. I turned and climbed the stairs to my bedroom. With each step, my body tightened. Jimmy would ruin my junior high school experience. I felt I'd always be attached to him. It was one thing to share the same last name, but we even shared the same first initial. People would ask me if he was my brother, or worse, my twin. They'd wonder why he was in the same homeroom with me if he was a year older. I shut the door, threw myself onto the bed and buried my face in the pillow.

My life was ruined. Now I'd have to look after Jimmy again.

Why me? Why couldn't Alison or Lynne have been close enough in age to go to the same school as Jimmy? This was my time! I was entering junior high and wanted to meet new friends from the other elementary schools who didn't know me as Jimmy's sister. I wanted to gossip and giggle on the way to school with girlfriends instead of walking next to Jimmy in silence. I didn't want to have to sit behind Jimmy in homeroom because *Poggi, Joyce* always followed *Poggi, James*. I didn't want to be glancing over my shoulder for Jimmy to make sure he didn't stare at pretty girls with his mouth wide open and saliva dripping from his lip or point too close to someone's face. I didn't want to scan the room every minute to make sure no one made fun of Jimmy, or me for that matter. I didn't want to run into him in the halls. I wanted to sit at the lunch table without worrying about where Jimmy might be sitting, if he was sitting alone, or if anyone was teasing him because he might have food on his face.

"What's wrong with you?" Lynne asked, plopping onto her bed and turning on the radio.

"Nothing."

Why would she care anyway? She was in high school and got to do whatever she wanted, always the first. I left the room and went outside because there wasn't any place in our house where I could really be alone.

How could I tell my mother I didn't want to be in the same homeroom with Jimmy? She'd be hurt, and it seemed cruel to Jimmy and selfish of me. As it was, Jimmy and I would start off each weekday morning together. We'd use the same bathroom, eat breakfast together, bump into each other, reach for our coats in the same closet usually at the same time, and walk to school together, shoulder to shoulder. My excitement about starting junior high plummeted.

A couple of days later, Mom guided me into the dining room by the elbow.

"I have something to tell you, Joyce."

I panicked about what I might have done wrong and hoped Mom wouldn't embarrass me with talk about puberty.

"Jimmy has been reassigned to homeroom 117," she informed me.

"What happened?" I asked, trying to conceal my relief.

"The school called to say there was a mix-up," she lied.

"A mix-up?" My jaw and shoulders relaxed. I stifled a secret smile yet still worried about Jimmy.

"Yes. Jimmy will be in room 117 and you will still be in room 116."

"Will he be okay in there?" I asked, wondering who'd look after him.

"Yes, Jimmy will be fine. It's all set," Mom assured me.

While most family decisions centered around Jimmy, I learned years later Mom made that seminal decision to separate us. The day after receiving the letters she had gone directly to the school and met with the principal. She gave me the fresh start I yearned for. Simultaneously, she risked giving Jimmy the independence he was not necessarily seeking. Mom would do it again more than twenty-five years later when she arranged for Jimmy to move to a supervised apartment. She and Dad made that momentous decision for many reasons. One reason was to avoid putting additional responsibility on any of the three daughters and their families.

Thanks to Mom's intervention, Jimmy sat one classroom away from me for the first five minutes of school each day. That gave me a sense of relief and freedom. Occasionally, I'd see him walk to the special education classroom at the other end of the first floor next to the nurse's office. He waded through a sea of loud, shuffling teenagers without a care. His locker was near the special ed classroom instead of with the kids in homeroom 117. Jimmy used the door near that classroom to leave school on his own at the end of the day, five minutes before the bell rang for the rest of the students.

Although I liked living close to school, I often wished for a longer walk home so I could be with a crowd of girls laughing and sharing secrets. On one hand, I wondered what they talked about and why I couldn't have fun like they did. On the other hand, I sensed a void next to me. It felt weird not to have Jimmy by my side. That void filled as soon as I walked through the back door. Jimmy would be sitting at the kitchen table with Oreos and a glass of milk.

"Hi Jimmy!" I'd say with a bit of envy knowing he'd gotten dismissed from school before me and was already snacking. He liked attending school around the corner instead of taking a bus to another school with a special ed classroom.

"Hi," he'd grunt with his mouth full while scraping chocolate crumbs off his lower lip with his upper teeth. His typical routine would become a relief in what was to become a tumultuous year for me as an adolescent.

Junior high brought more firsts than I imagined. My jaw dropped the first time I saw Cathy McKallagat's breasts in the girls' shower room after gym class. Sagging near her waist, they were the largest things I'd ever seen. She was a seventh-grader like me but appeared womanly.

I had a full frontal view of Cathy who had mousy-brown

hair draping both sides of her oily face. She fastened her bra in front under her breasts. Her bra had not two, but three hooks—the kind grandmothers buy in J.C. Penney's. Blue veins squiggled down each pendulous breast. Dark brown saucers encircled nipples pointing directly at me. I froze, wide-eyed with amazement as Cathy twisted the bra around her torso and deposited her melons into the unpadded harness. I easily reached my arms around me to clasp the stretchy A-cup padded bra and cover the two mosquito bites on my chest. How had Cathy's chest grown so big by the tender age of twelve? If she was thirteen, a year older than me, then there might still be hope for me.

To get ready for gym class, you had to sprint to the girls' locker room, change into your uniform and sit cross-legged at a designated post in the gym within four minutes. I maneuvered past the crowd of pimply, gangly classmates at various stages of undress. Arms flailed while we shared one long wooden and often slippery bench. Luckily, my locker was an end unit that came in handy because it offered more elbow room and privacy. I hid my budding body and turned toward the wall when changing.

Our gym uniform should have been featured as a "Don't" in *Glamour* magazine. The two-piece, royal blue ensemble made of thick, stiff cotton was the ugliest and most uncomfortable piece of clothing a teenage girl could wear in 1969. The cap-sleeved shirtdress snapped from collar to hip requiring the wearer to step into it. It flared out and made the hips and thighs appear larger—perfect for the teenage girl who wanted to accentuate those parts of her body. Bulky matching bloomers had elastic that dug into the waist and upper thighs. School policy required our name be embroidered across the chest and across the butt.

I suppose this was important in case our gym teacher wanted to yell at us when struggling to climb up those prickly thick ropes to the gym ceiling.

As soon as we finished the madness of changing into our uniforms, we were required to sit in position on the floor so the teacher could take attendance. Along the far wall of the girls' side of the gymnasium, numbers were painted from one to ten. On the adjoining wall, where the teacher stood in front of the locker room door, capital letters were painted A through F. My assigned position was F7.

Now if you happened to be menstruating on the day of your gym class, you were required to stand in position, not sit. This enabled the teacher to easily note you as excused from the mandatory shower at the end of class. As if it weren't humiliating enough to broadcast to all your classmates that your "friend" was there, if the partitions were open to the boys' side of the gym, then they also learned the breaking news that it was that time of the month for you.

Pear-shaped Miss Talena, armed with her clipboard, paced the floor with a duck walk, ready to take attendance. She wore khaki boy shorts, a button-down camp shirt with her ever-present whistle looped around her neck, sturdy sneakers, and no make-up. Leaning forward, she raised her head to see who was standing, calling out positions:

"A3." Check. "D5." Check. "E2." Check.

"F7 . . . is that you back there, Joyce?" she asked craning her neck.

"Yes," I whimpered.

Dear Lord, let me crawl somewhere and hide. I dared not make eye contact with anyone as I felt blood surge to my face. Hurry up already and make the darn check mark so I can sit down before the boys notice.

Class began with as much enthusiasm as was needed to listen to the principal lecture about parking lot safety. Except for the few females who possessed the natural ability to perform anything athletic, the majority of us stumbled our way through field hockey, basketball, tennis, gymnastics, dodge ball, medicine ball passes, and running around the outdoor track until Miss Talena couldn't bear watching our clumsy, pitiful performance any longer. I didn't really feel like I was learning anything athletic, nor did I care. I certainly wasn't aiming to break a sweat. Still, I had to suffer through the curricular requirement, all the while worrying about the impending, final frightful shower scene.

"Hit the showers!" yelled Miss Talena after blowing her whistle at the end of every class. Except for my menstruating sisters, we'd all scurry to our lockers, strip down to our bras and panties, and run barefooted to the showers. Menstruating girls had the option of taking a private shower in one of two separate stalls. At that age, no one wanted to stand out by being isolated from the norm so those private showers remained unused.

A ledge about four feet high outside one wall of the communal shower area had a row of about thirty hooks for our underwear. This was where we removed our bras and panties, took our school-issued, undersized towels and, holding them above our heads, ran through the adjoining corridor of water spraying us from both sides. No washing, lathering, or anything else vaguely resembling cleaning the body happened there. We'd rush through, hoping not to slip on the tile or ruin our hair and make-up. Inevitably, a logjam occurred at the end of the shower because Miss Talena planted herself there, clipboard in hand. Each naked girl was required to state her attendance position so our dispassionate teacher could check off that we did, indeed, take a shower.

"Girls, take your time," she'd say.

Miss Talena was in no hurry. Sometimes she'd take a little longer to put a check mark next to the name of tall, blonde Mindy Gleed. She once commented to Mindy about her developing new curves. Although I felt certain Miss Talena wouldn't single me out that way, the thought disgusted me.

It was easy to see Miss Talena favored the athletic girls. At field hockey tryouts, I got cut in the first round. Same for basketball. Even though I yearned to be a member of a team, competitive sports really didn't excite me. The only other activity for girls my junior high school offered was cheerleading which didn't require much physical aptitude other than doing cartwheels and splits. It meant being on a team without playing a sport. Cut the first year, I made it my second year. Okay, I sort of liked the recognition. The cherry and gray pleated skirt and matching sweater with a felt megaphone across the chest was a cute outfit. Still, cheerleaders never got their names or pictures in the paper for scoring points in a game. Nor did they win championships or trophies.

Just once I wanted to win something. It dawned on me that I wasn't an outstanding talent—on the ball field, on the stage, or in the classroom. I didn't know how I would ever get an award or be recognized for anything other than being Jimmy's sister.

15

I had never won anything. My station in life was the middle of the pack. That was my role—to be in the middle, second, invisible.

Every semester, I missed qualifying for Distinguished Honor Roll and had to settle for Honor Roll. My name was buried in a column of the *Delaware County News* with a long list of other kids. I sang alto in the chorus but didn't qualify for the Ensemble, a select group of girls, mostly sopranos, who stayed on key. When I auditioned for the school play, the director cut me. Clearly my acting ability wasn't up to snuff either.

I saw a chance for recognition with Miss Shalit, my homeroom and English teacher. She announced a contest for the best recitation of the Gettysburg Address by all seventh graders. Public speaking wasn't something I'd imagine myself doing since I generally preferred staying in the background, but my love of words took me out of my comfort zone.

With determination, I practiced President Lincoln's address in my room, in the shower, in front of the bathroom mirror, walking to school, lying in bed at night. Over and over again I said to myself:

Fourscore and seven years ago our fathers brought forth upon this continent a new nation, conceived in liberty and dedicated to the proposition that all men are created equal.

Selected as one of the top two students to represent my homeroom, I advanced to the second round of thirty-six before qualifying in the top ten of all seventh graders. With each private recitation, I got a rush, stood taller, and fantasized that maybe I really could win the competition. If the field hockey coach doubted I could score a goal and the drama director determined I couldn't act, then I'd get up on stage and surprise everyone by speaking with confidence.

Before the Wednesday morning assembly began, I peeked from behind the velvet stage curtain into the audience and spied the judges: three male history teachers from the senior high school, seated in the first row. I noticed the other contestants' mothers seated in the back row of the auditorium before the students filed in, and realized I made a mistake by telling Mom not to bother coming. She'd asked me if she should attend and I told her the assembly was for students only (which I assumed was the case), so she made other plans. Jimmy sat out there somewhere so at least I had one family member watching.

At the time, I assumed Jimmy had no understanding of the speech. Although he would have known Lincoln had been a U.S. President, in-depth studying about the Civil War would have been above his intellectual capability. He had a cursory understanding of slavery and grasped why "all men are created equal" inasmuch as they all got a chance, they all got a turn.

I, on the other hand, was questioning the concept of equality. If all men were created equal, then why was my brother born with a mental disability? Why were some boys in the smarter classes? Who chose the boys to run the audio-visual equipment? Why did some men have more money, fancier cars, and bigger homes than others? Furthermore, why were men in charge of everything—at banks, schools, and stores? Why did I only see male doctors who gave direction to female nurses and secretaries? Where were the women and why weren't they in leadership positions? The only women of authority I witnessed were teachers, and even then, they reported to a male principal. Why wasn't a female teacher judging the competition?

The contestants drew numbers and I was second in the line-up. I felt confident in the outfit Mom selected for me: a sunflower yellow, long-sleeved top with the zipper from bosom to neck (zipped all the way up), paired with a brown and gold Navajo print skirt, nude stockings and brown, low-heeled shoes. My shoulder-length hair was neatly combed and pulled away from my face with a tortoise shell barrette.

"Now make sure you stand up straight and keep your hands by your side," Mom reminded me. She hadn't a clue how much I'd practiced and how badly I wanted to win. I was afraid if she knew, I'd be jinxed. I never practiced in front of her because she'd tell me how to revise and enunciate. I'd feel pressured to recite it her way, not mine.

However, I knew Miss Shalit would be rooting for me since I was her homeroom representative. I wanted to please my favorite teacher who always dressed in stylish clothes and who spoke with perfect diction from glossy pink lips. I approached her desk the morning of the competition.

"Miss Shalit, I've been practicing a lot, but what if I forget the lines when I get to the auditorium and see all those people?"

"Joyce, you can do this," she said, settling her thick mascara eyes on me. "I want you to project your voice when you get on stage. Speak clearly and loudly. Be confident. I know you'll do great."

I eagerly waited my turn backstage, bouncing at the knees. Finally, I heard my name.

"Our next student is Joyce Poggi."

Walking to the center of the stage, up there all by myself I saw a crowd but no faces. A restless hum layered the auditorium. I took a deep breath, paused for a moment and began:

Fourscore and seven years ago . . .

Oh boy, I was definitely on top of my game. I got myself into a mental zone and projected the strong words that would have made even President Lincoln proud.

. . . dedicated to the proposition . . .

As each word emerged from my lips, I grew taller and stronger.

. . . the last full measure of devotion . . .

Those important, multi-syllabic words made me feel credible and smart in front of all my classmates. Within two minutes, my speech was completed.

. . . shall not perish from the earth.

My chest collapsed with happy relief. I curtsied and exited stage left, grinning to my competitors while reveling in the applause I knew was for me alone. A chill ran down my spine. I had nailed it. No one could come close to me.

The remaining students recited the speech as I watched and listened backstage. After the fourth recitation, the audience squirmed in their seats. The tenth competitor finished and the judges huddled to choose the winner.

Five minutes later, the judges presented their decision to the principal. All ten competitors filed back on stage and lined up in order of recitation for the results. My chest fluttered inside. I was desperate to hear my name called. Is this how the Miss America contestants felt?

After a few words, the principal made his announcement.

"The winner is . . ." imaginary drum roll here . . . "Nancy

Hamill."

Applause erupted in the auditorium. Nancy? She had "ums" in her speech and kept tucking her hair behind her ear. Instead of standing up straight, she bent her knee and posed like Betty Boop. Applause! Nancy stepped forward to receive congratulations from the principal and three judges, all men. She shook their hands and accepted the plaque and a book about Abraham Lincoln. Applause! My knees went weak. It took a concerted effort to clap and keep the fake smile on my face. I was deeply hurt and felt betrayed.

"There are second and third place winners, too," said the principal. "Second place goes to Joyce Poggi."

My name! That's me! I'll concede it did feel good, but not great. I wanted my name called as the winner, not runner-up. Meek, obligatory applause for me. I stepped forward to receive a wimpy handshake and thought, *That's it?* I hesitated, looked around and realized no plaque or award would be presented to me. A clumsy handshake was my only reward for weeks of private rehearsals in the shower.

Not to revel in the honor of second place too long, the principal announced the third place winner, which meant I should get back in line. I returned to the middle of the line, empty-handed.

"Third place goes to Vahan Sagherian." Hoots, cheers and whistles ensued for Vahan. Everyone loved Vahan, a short, smart, likable kid with a unique accent. There I was, stuck in the middle again, sandwiched between the winner and the fan favorite.

After the assembly, photos were snapped in the school lobby. The photographer told us to get closer. I wanted to grab the plaque and book out of Nancy's hands. For the rest of the school day, I privately sulked over second place. I couldn't concentrate in class because the loss hurt too much.

When I arrived home, Mom greeted me at the front door with a smile and a hug.

"Congratulations!"

"I didn't win, Mom." Why was she congratulating me?

"Yes, you did. You came in second place," she said proudly. "Mrs. DeStefano called me to say all the parents agreed you should have won."

"She did?" Although Mom intended to make me feel better, she made me feel worse, like I'd been cheated.

"Yes. Mrs. DeStefano said you were the clear winner."

I dropped my books on the dining room chair and pretended to be happy for Mom, but couldn't.

The sting worsened when Lynne arrived home from school.

"I heard the girl in the mini dress won," she reported. Gossip at the senior high was that the three male history teachers sat in the front row of the auditorium and favored Nancy, who sidled across the stage in a baby-girl mini dress no one had ever seen before.

The naïve teen in me couldn't have guessed that the judges would ignore objectivity in favor of sexism. Their actions confirmed to me that young women were judged first on appearance. Oratory skill and intelligence were secondary. The painful lesson would alert me to more unfairness in the world— beyond what was unfair for Jimmy. I'd face inequity when it came time for opportunities in high school and college. More significantly, as a professional woman entering the workplace in the late 1970s, I'd have to assert myself. One female manager advised me early in my career to fight for what I wanted. "Be aggressive," she said. "Don't play the back court. Go to the net."

The incongruous lesson I learned from the junior high competition was that all men were not created equal. Some were born brain-damaged and didn't get the opportunities of able-minded men. Furthermore, all women weren't created equal. Worse, men and women were not created equal.

"Joyce came in second place," said Mom to Lynne in an encouraging tone.

"Oh, really?" said Lynne. "That's great, Joyce. They didn't say who came in second."

Of course they didn't. Who cares about second place? Does anyone ever remember the Olympic silver medalist? Does anyone care about the runner-up to Miss America or the semi-finalist in any competition?

After I cleared the dinner dishes away from the table, Mom kept at it.

"Joyce, since Daddy and I weren't at the assembly, recite the Gettysburg Address for us now."

"Now? Here?" I asked, holding the plates.

"Yes, for Daddy and me. We want to hear it."

"No, I don't want to."

"Oh, c'mon. For us?"

"No, Mom. It's over."

I left the kitchen. Any hint of a stage or oratory career for me died that afternoon. That night, in front of the bathroom mirror and later, lying in my bed, I continued to recite President Lincoln's speech to myself, putting emphasis on different words, for what might have been the winning performance.

Before I drifted off to sleep, Mom tiptoed into the room I shared with Lynne and Alison. She sat on the edge of my bed and put her warm hands on my cheeks.

"You were the best speaker on stage today," she said in a

soothing voice. "Mrs. DeStefano told me so and I believe her."

"No, I wasn't. I didn't win."

"Joyce, honey, you will have to be content within yourself, knowing you were the best in the competition," she said. She kissed my forehead, tucked the covers close to my body and turned out the light. Mom loved imparting words of wisdom but her tidbit sounded empty and strange to me. Content within myself? If I didn't win awards, how would anyone know me as an accomplished person?

I lost my thoughts when I heard Jimmy crooning from his bedroom, repeating lyrics from the Fifth Dimension hit song for all the family to hear:

Let the sunshine. Let the sunshine in.

The sunshine in.

Let the sunshine. Let the sunshine in.

The sunshine in.

Jimmy distracted me from wallowing in self-pity and it annoyed me. How could he be so happy when I felt miserable?

The following week my photo made the *Delaware County News*, the local weekly. There I was, standing next to the winner of the Gettysburg Address contest, still feeling like a sorry second.

It would take me decades to unravel the truth in my mother's words and find a way toward a sense of contentment and self-acceptance.

16

Jimmy ambled on the outside, closer to the street. Mom and Dad taught him it was the gentlemanly way. On cold winter mornings, we tightened our lips, shaped our mouths into an oval, and slowly exhaled.

"I see my breath!" exclaimed Jimmy grinning on our one-mile walk to Upper Darby Senior High.

At five foot ten, Jimmy was in the eleventh grade, a year ahead of me at the large public school with almost three thousand students in the tenth, eleventh, and twelfth grades. He had been assigned to the special education class, learning with other kids who had a variety of developmental disabilities.

Jimmy and I chose to walk on the north side of heavily traveled State Road. A stone wall bordered Arlington Cemetery on the south side. I disliked walking on that side because it felt eerie with row after row of tombstones. Just as bad was the dog poop on the pavement. Some dog owners didn't pick up the mess, so it became an obstacle course requiring pedestrians to constantly look downward and zigzag their stride.

Along the way, Jimmy and I never talked much. We were in different worlds. His interests included the Philadelphia Flyers and the Sixers. I preferred my English classes, cheerleading, and obsessing about my manicured fingernails. Acne was a major preoccupation and I'd hoped Phisoderm skin cleanser and Clearasil would be my miracle cures. Jimmy had teenage acne too, but he was happy about learning how to shave. Despite our diverging paths, a bond existed between us. It was as if an invisible, elastic band connected us. We were always tethered to each other even when he wasn't bumping into me.

The invisible elastic band would stretch whenever I urged him to keep up with me as we hurried across busy State Road. I worried someday he'd be distracted or move too slowly and get hit by a car while I moved ahead. I envisioned turning and seeing him lying in the street. I couldn't live with myself if something bad had happened to Jimmy especially while he was in my care. Nevertheless, he remained near me faithfully, usually behind by a step or two. He possessed the predictable and frequent knack of tripping on the heel of my foot. He'd apologize as I'd bend my knee and glance over my shoulder to check if my shoe was scuffed or if I'd gotten a run in my nylon stocking.

"You 'kay? You 'kay? 'kay, Joyce?" he'd ask tapping my shoulder. He had a big heart but couldn't help being clumsy. It never occurred to me then that Jimmy had a protective instinct as big brother. I always considered myself the protector. I'd learn later never to underestimate his feelings or judgment. Once he began living away from our parents, Jimmy intuited a lot more about our family dynamics than he ever let on previously. He gained more confidence expressing himself well into his fifties.

Once across State Road, we'd walk by V&B, our favorite deli where Jimmy would often linger and stare in the window.

"Ooh, Tastykakes, Joyce," he'd say tapping the window.

"C'mon, Jimmy," I'd say tugging his sleeve. "We'll be late for school. Besides, we only have enough money for lunch."

The last stretch of our walk required cutting through a parking lot behind the Dairy Queen, where the Warlocks (or, as Mom called them, the Drexel Hill hoods) hung out.

"Keep walking, Jimmy. Don't look at them and don't stop," I'd say.

"Uh-kay."

Positioning myself between the Warlocks and Jimmy, I breathed more evenly once we passed, never daring to look back. Instead of waiting at the traffic light, we risked crossing dangerous Lansdowne Avenue and walked the last hundred yards up the hill to school. Once there, Jimmy went his way and I went mine. We rarely saw each other in the hallways, although I was always on the lookout for him because I didn't want him to stand out and get teased. I had to be ready to diffuse a problem or pull him aside to tell him to tuck in his shirt or close his mouth and stop drooling.

One afternoon, as I sauntered toward my locker, I noticed a commotion at the row of lockers beyond mine. There stood another gang in black leather jackets and Jimmy was with them. A lump formed in my throat. I could tell they were pestering him. Jimmy gave them his awkward smile and cautious laugh that signaled discomfort. He wanted so badly to be part of a group, any group. He trusted people and didn't realize that someone might try to befriend him for an ulterior motive. My intuition told me those jerks were trying to get money from him. He was defenseless in a sea of teenage cruelty. One thug nudged Jimmy and another held his hand out as they boxed him in. A surge of adrenaline rose up in me.

I rushed up to the group in my pleated cheerleader skirt and letter sweater. I squared my shoulders and stood as tall as I could in my five-feet-four inch frame with my books as armor held tightly against my chest.

"The retard's sister," one sneered as he elbowed a friend. It wasn't the first time I'd been called that. It stung every single time.

I summoned strength I didn't know I had, tightened my lips around clenched teeth, and glowered. The brutes dispersed as I neared Jimmy, denying me the chance to give them a piece of my mind, even though I wasn't sure what I was going to say. For the first time in my life, I realized the impact of my silent presence. The intoxicating rush of power was something I liked and wanted to experience again.

"Jimmy," I said, "what did those guys want?"

As he studied the floor, Jimmy replied softly, "Nothing."

"Jimmy! Tell me." My eyes searched his. "What did they want? Did they try to get money from you?"

Lifting his gaze, he said, "Yeah, but I didn't give them any, Joyce."

"Good, Jimmy. The next time that happens you walk away and ignore those guys. They're creeps."

"Yeah, they're creeps. They're creeps."

"I'll see you later." I touched his arm, reassuringly. "Jimmy! Be careful. And don't ever give money to anyone!"

Jimmy tapped his pants pocket, turned and left me standing alone at the locker. I slowly exhaled.

Although Jimmy is wary when first meeting people, he wants to trust them. He wants to believe that strangers are genuine when they try to befriend him. He once sold his golf clubs to a co-worker for five dollars. When Dad found out, he contacted the employer and got the clubs back. A roommate once offered to cut Jimmy's hair for less money than the barbershop. Jimmy knew something was amiss because he told us about it. At my urging, the staff of the supervised apartment discovered the roommate had a sketchy history and they removed him. A worker at the convenience store where Jimmy buys his coffee encouraged him to return on Thanksgiving to meet a woman who would take him to her house. When he told me, alarm bells sounded and I had to explain to him why he couldn't go. Again, he instinctively knew something wasn't right but yearned for what he hoped would be sincere companionship.

To this day, my sisters and I constantly remind him to guard his wallet and never lend or give money to anyone. He's heard us because he barely leaves a tip at the diner nor does he ever treat us to an ice cream cone. Whenever he visits Lynne, Alison or me, we take him shopping, golfing, and out to eat. He knows we're pushovers. He usually returns home with the same amount of cash in his wallet or more and still his parting words are often "Do you have any money for me?"

As my confidence grew at school, I paid closer attention when my father discussed politics and world events around the kitchen table. After Dad finished his dinner, I'd bring him a package of graham crackers and coffee for dessert. He'd break the crackers on the perforated line, dunk two small rectangles into the coffee, tap them on the side of his cup and, without looking up, ask a question.

"Who are Woodward and Bernstein and why are they important?"

Crackers to lips, he scanned the table and waited for an answer.

"Something to do with Watergate," I said.

"Right. What?" Without the answer, he continued, "Why

does everyone want to know who Deep Throat is?"

Deep Throat. I bowed my head and blushed. I couldn't imagine why Dad would mention the name of a porn star at the dinner table. I could barely say the word "period" out loud even when talking about grammar and he wanted me to explain Deep Throat?

Dad talked about Nixon's cabinet as if they were high school rivals before a big football game: This one's a liar, that one's an idiot, the other one can't tell his right foot from his left. Transfixed by the news, Dad delighted in all the Washington shenanigans, especially when the rich and powerful got caught.

"Lies, lies, lies," he said. "These guys are all liars."

I remembered lying about the hitchhiking incident and the time I forged Mom's signature on a geometry test. I thought about dating a football player whom I didn't even like because I wanted to fit in and be recognized as a couple by my classmates. I'd been trying unsuccessfully to shed my goody two-shoes persona. My gut told me how wrong it all was.

"Remember," Dad said, tearing a piece of Italian bread at the dinner table one winter night. "If you tell one lie, then you have to tell another, then another and another. Before you know it, they all pile up. Pretty soon, you start believing your lies. Eventually, you wind up like these crooks and get caught."

Later that night I told my parents about a party being held on the other side of the tracks and asked if I could go. I didn't know the host and had a gut feeling the party would get out of hand. I worried the police would show up and there'd be arrests for underage drinking and marijuana. I searched for any excuse not to go. Dad must have detected the apprehension in my voice and face as he stood in the front hall for a moment.

"Okay. You can go to the party. I trust your judgment."

His words hit me hard and echoed in my head repeatedly. For years, I'd hear his voice saying, "I trust your judgment." I wanted him to ask me questions to which I'd have to answer "I don't know" so he would refuse to let me leave the house. But Dad didn't because he trusted me.

Stopped dead in my tracks, I did a slow about-face and lingered in the dining room. Pacing and sweating, I chewed my cuticles trying to figure out what to do. How could I continue to deceive my parents? I'd have to keep lying. And I'd already lied about this sketchy gang I'd been with–all because I wanted to be seen dating a cute football player a year older than me. I was completely out of place with him and his seedy group of friends and knew it. But as a naive teenager desperate for a boyfriend, I wasn't thinking clearly.

I wanted to separate myself from that crowd, but didn't know how to do it. Dad's voice kept ringing in my ear, "Lies, lies, lies . . ." and "I trust your judgment." I covered my face with my hands in shame, took a couple of deep breaths and swallowed hard. It seemed as if another person had been occupying my body during that lying season.

Upstairs I heard Jimmy repeating one of his favorite songs from the band Steam:

Nah, nah, nah, nah,

Nah, nah, nah, nah,

Hey, hey / Goodbye.

I climbed the stairs, called my ride with an excuse, and changed into my pajamas. I stayed in my room for the rest of the night.

"They're all going down," said Dad the next morning about Nixon's circle of friends, the CREEP (Committee to Re-Elect the President). "You know," he said from the couch, lowering the newspaper to meet my eyes. "You are who you associate with."

I tried concealing a sigh of relief, happy to be back on the straight and narrow.

Nah, nah, nah, nah,

Nah, nah, nah, nah,

Hey, hey / Goodbye.

After that I didn't care about having a boyfriend. I wasn't part of any popular crowd nor did I make it as an athlete, musician, or thespian. So I immersed myself in schoolwork taking particular interest in English classes. I was an average student who happened to be a cheerleader who only enjoyed the limelight while cheering at basketball and football games. I didn't smoke, drink, or cause trouble. Is there anything more boring than someone who's middle of the road?

Although I yearned for some recognition, the middle represented safe territory for me. And always, in the back of my mind, I had this feed running: to be responsible and an ethical role model because of Jimmy. I knew my parents constantly worried about Jimmy and his future, so I assumed I had to be quiet and obedient and exemplary to make things easier for them. Then they wouldn't have to worry about me. Instead, maybe I could make them proud. Maybe they'd smile more often instead of knitting their brows.

17

Jimmy shuffled through the house with his thick fingers curled around the white driver's ed booklet. Although a few months had passed since he turned sixteen, it didn't appear as if Mom or Dad planned to teach him how to drive.

"What if he's in an accident and gets hurt?" I overheard Mom say to Dad one day.

"Accidents happen, Ro."

"I'm scared, Babe. Besides, what about the insurance?" she asked. "Will he even get insured? What if he crashes the car, injures someone, and we get sued?"

Dad remained wordless. He knew he'd never win the argument. Although Jimmy knew how to follow rules and read street signs, Mom and Dad feared Jimmy might not be able to pass the written portion of the test.

It turns out Jimmy never asked my father to teach him to drive. Deep down, my brother must have had doubts himself. I don't know whom it pained more—Jimmy or my parents—to know an important adolescent milestone, learning to drive, wouldn't be met. Furthermore, it signaled Jimmy's continuing dependence on others in his adulthood. He'd have to rely on my parents, sisters, and me for rides to work, doctor appointments, and social events for the rest of his life.

When I turned sixteen twenty months later, I tiptoed into Jimmy's room and grabbed the booklet from his nightstand. I took it back to my bedroom and started studying. Not long after, Jimmy spotted me reading the book. I overheard him pleading to Mom and Dad.

"I'm seventeen!" he said. "She's sixteen. I'm older than her. I should be driving first, not her." I heard the scrape of a kitchen chair and then heard the swinging door between the kitchen and dining room swoosh closed—my mother's attempt to contain an argument.

I knew Dad had mixed feelings and would have taught Jimmy even if it meant more than the required training hours. But Mom never had any intention of letting Jimmy get behind the wheel.

Then my turn came. With my learner's permit in hand, Dad took me out in our 1971 Country Squire station wagon with wood paneling on the sides. Dad remained remarkably patient with me behind the wheel. I found this interesting because he was typically impatient when driving, always switching lanes, hurrying to "keep up" with the guy in front of him, and occasionally cursing other drivers for their ineptitude. We went cruising all over Drexel Hill after mastering several sessions on the usual training ground–the junior high school parking lot.

One Saturday morning, Dad broke from reading the latest Watergate news and decided I was ready for the test.

"You finished all your driver training classes?"

"Yes. At school."

"Then what are we waiting for? Let's go!" he said, folding the newspaper.

"Now? Today?" I asked, following him out of the living room, half-smiling in anticipation despite the flutter in my chest.

"Why not?" he said, heading for the back door.

He put on his coat, took the keys from the key rack and tossed them to me.

"C'mon. Get your coat."

"But it's raining."

"Oh, for Pete's sake, it's drizzling."

"Dad," I confessed on the way to the test center. "I practiced the three-point turn only once and I'm afraid it'll be the reason I fail the test."

"Pull in over here," he said without hesitation, pointing to the parking lot of the Springfield Mall. "That's it. Turn right here and you can practice before we get there."

I wanted to see if I could turn that ark around without backing up more than once. Dad uncharacteristically relaxed in the passenger seat, amused at the sights from his vantage point.

"You're ready now," Dad said after I completed the three-point turn without incident.

"Shouldn't I try it again? Keep practicing?"

"Nah, you're ready. Let's go."

At the crowded DMV exam center, I filled out the paperwork and waited. I prayed for a nice female examiner while sitting next to Dad and drumming my fingers on my thighs. As I imagined buying a new wallet for my license, I heard my name called. Dad winked as I left him in the lobby with other anxious parents. I slid into the station wagon, buckled my seat belt, and waited.

The passenger door opened and I spotted a belt buckle at the center of a protruding belly. A portly, middle-aged guy plopped himself onto the passenger side of the bench seat, forcing me upward an inch or two. I prepared to turn on the ignition, but he jutted out his hand between us and informed me the process would begin with an oral examination. I answered a few questions. Thankfully, none were about what to do when approaching a school bus, which, for some reason, I couldn't get straight.

"All right. Begin," he said. "Start the car." Mr. Portly gave me curt instructions. Drive down here. Turn left. Drive ahead here. Back up. Park in this space.

"Now I want you to drive through the cones on this imaginary road," he instructed.

Please don't let me knock over any orange cones, I prayed, turning the wheel left and right, left and right. The markers, at the time, appeared closer than I suspect they really were. Lastly, the dreaded three-point turn.

"Okay, you're done. Now drive over to the administration building and pull into the first spot," he said pointing. With newfound confidence, I breathed a sigh of relief and dreamed about driving to the Springfield Mall that afternoon all by myself while Mr. Portly wrote on his clipboard.

Stone-faced, he said without a preamble, "You failed. Try again next week."

I stared at him with my mouth agape.

"You failed to maintain a consistent speed on the serpentine road," he soberly replied. As I sat there slumped and speechless, he unbuckled his seat belt and got out of the car. My side of the station wagon descended along with my enthusiasm.

I don't fail tests. I've never failed a test at school and now this? Lynne passed on her first try and I didn't?

Within minutes, my father appeared in the same seat with a smile on his face.

"So?" he asked with an optimistic huff.

"I failed."

"You failed?" he said in a voice of disbelief, pronouncing the word failed with two syllables.

"He said I failed to maintain a consistent speed on the serpentine road."

"Oh, for God's sake." Dad paused a moment and then ordered me to switch seats. Peering out the passenger side window at droplets of rain pinging my window, my lips quivered. Dad informed me years later that he found the situation comical and restrained himself from laughing on the ride home.

The next week Dad took me back for a second try and I passed.

Since Mom drove the wagon and Dad drove a Volkswagen Bug, to increase my chances of using a car, I decided to learn how to drive a stick shift on the VW. Once again, Dad happily agreed to teach me. Although occasionally confusing the clutch with the stick, I warmed up with lessons in the junior high parking lot. Then I graduated to State Road and the residential streets of our town, known for a stop sign at virtually every corner.

"Turn right onto Bond Avenue, honey," Dad directed. "Then I want you to take a left onto Cobbs Street."

"Cobbs?" I asked to be sure. "There's parking on both sides of that street."

"I know that," he laughed.

Although I'd been on that road hundreds of times, I never imagined driving the route myself. Cobbs Street was a narrow, one-way street crowded with twin homes and cars parked end to end on both sides. At the top of the Cobbs Street incline was a four-lane highway, the busiest road near my neighborhood where cars drove by at lightning speed.

My anxiety increased as adrenaline rushed through me. I knew Dad would never put me in a dangerous situation, but I couldn't shake the fear of falling backwards. I envisioned the car rolling down the hill sideswiping the parked cars. It'd be like going backward down a giant sliding board in a two-thousand-pound bumper car. The screeching of metal against metal would sound a hundred times worse than nails on a blackboard. Paint and shards would litter the street like confetti. Our insurance rates would go through the roof and I'd never be able to drive again.

At the top of Cobbs Street, my right leg pressed down hard on the brake while my left leg pressed down on the clutch. The sensation of both heels off the floor kept me alert as I pressed for dear life.

"Put the stick in neutral and you can take your foot off the clutch," Dad said.

"That's my left foot, right?" I asked.

"Right, your left foot," he confirmed as I processed his response. I took a few breaths while beads of sweat accumulated around my hairline.

"Now we're gonna turn right. Put it in first gear."

"It won't go."

"You gotta press down the clutch first!" he said with a half laugh.

"I am," I answered, trying to coax the stick to move forward left.

"The clutch! The clutch! On the floor is the clutch, and this is the stick, remember?" he said cradling my right hand over the stick shift with his fleshy left hand.

Perched precariously at the top of that concrete mountain, contemplating whether Daddy and I would be riding in an ambulance soon, I couldn't concentrate. We'd be on the six o'clock news and a photo of our mangled Beetle would be featured in the *Delaware County News*.

Finally, I pressed down the clutch. Dad leaned over to check my feet. "You gotta press the clutch all the way down, *all the way down*, before you can put the car in gear. Keep your right foot on the brake. Now move the stick into first gear, and then slowly release the clutch."

I took my foot off the brake. Dad yelled, "The clutch! The clutch!"

Oops, wrong foot.

"That's it," he said. "Let it out slowly. When you start to hear the engine grind, then put your foot on the gas . . . slowly!" The whir of cars racing in front of me distracted me, as did the anticipation of vehicles that would eventually drive up behind the car. My anxiety increased and I sweated at the thought of Dad and me squeezed into a little blue capsule of metal.

"But when I get ready to put my foot on the accelerator, the car will roll backward if I take my foot off the brake," I said.

"No it won't," he said. "Do it quickly."

The car jerked forward, taking Daddy's and my body with it in similar motion, then jerked backward and stalled.

"Brake! Clutch! You let the clutch out too fast!"

I checked the rearview mirror and prayed no one would drive up the hill behind me. Every inch of my body tensed. Dad brought me back to reality with his strong, soothing voice. "Try again. Slowly."

So many instructions. So many movements to make. Another stall.

"Again," said Dad. I checked the rearview mirror and saw a car driving up. A third stall. My body constricted. Gripping the steering wheel tightly, the hair on my forearms lifted from the skin. Would I ever get off this incline? I hoped the guy in the car behind me wouldn't get too close.

As if clairvoyant, Dad said, "Never mind the guy behind you. You can do it. Remember what I said. Release the clutch slowly."

Inhale, exhale. C'mon Joyce, you can do this. Focus! Otherwise, the police will arrive to write up an accident report after you've crashed into the car behind you. Finally, the fourth time was a charm.

"Way to go!" Dad said.

"I did it!" I said banging the steering wheel. My whole body felt lighter.

Mom let me borrow the station wagon to drive to basketball games where I was a cheerleader. On weekends, Dad let me drive the Volkswagen Bug. I didn't mind the fact that it was a little dirty inside. The VW was like an adult toy. Feeling more confident about my stick shift skills by the time I commuted to college, I regularly barreled down Old Lane, the one-way street parallel to Cobbs Street, also with parking on both sides. I'd downshift into second gear and glide through four stop signs before pulling into our driveway on Penn Avenue with a sigh of relief not to have seen a police cruiser parked around any corner.

Besides helping Mom with errands to the grocery store, sometimes I drove Jimmy and Alison around town when Lynne was working. One Saturday, when Jimmy was my only passenger in the station wagon, I turned into the empty parking lot of the junior high school.

"What are we doing?" Jimmy asked when I stopped the car.

"Do you want to drive?" I asked him, raising my eyebrows

and smiling.

He chuckled apprehensively. "Drive? Me?"

"Yes, you."

"Uh, I don't know . . ."

"Do you want to try?"

"Uh . . . Uh-kay. I'll try it." Jimmy knew the rules required having a learner's permit and an experienced driver with you before getting behind the wheel.

"You can do it, Jimmy. I'll help you. It's easy," I said. "It will be our secret."

I threw the car into park and told him to slide over while I ran around the back of the wagon and took his place in the passenger seat. Jimmy giggled and picked at his knuckles when anxious. They reminded me of miniature pitcher mounds. I felt jittery, too. Not about getting caught, only about crashing the family car.

I told Jimmy to put his foot on the brake and shift the car into drive.

"Okay, you can go now."

Jimmy put his foot on the accelerator as I instructed him to . . . *Whoosh!* We lurched forward. Suddenly I was the one laughing nervously. I could tell he felt in control and out of control at the same time. His hands gripped the wheel and turned it about five degrees back and forth, back and forth.

"Like this, Joyce?"

"Not quite. Put your foot on the brake," I said. His size twelve Converse jammed the brake and we came to a sudden stop. "Try it again, Jimmy. Press the pedal lightly this time and go straight. Hold the wheel still."

He paused.

"No one is around," I said motioning to the empty lot. "We

won't get hurt because there's all this space."

Jimmy knew his limits, though. After the second or third acceleration, he stopped the car. He turned and stared at me without saying a word. I knew how badly he wanted to drive, but could see the fear in his face.

"That was good, Jimmy. We'll try again another time," I reassured him.

I really wanted to teach my brother how to drive. I wanted to train Jimmy on something that neither Mom nor Dad were willing to risk. In doing so, I'd prove to them Jimmy's capability and mine as well, as the teacher who showed confidence in him. I'd alleviate a burden for my parents and they'd be proud of both Jimmy and me. I wanted to see the pride in Jimmy's face and feel the satisfaction knowing I had something to do with it.

At the same time, I knew Jimmy would never get a chance to be in the driver's seat—for anything. My younger life was already accelerating past my older brother's. That's not the way it was supposed to be. An older brother was supposed to do things first and maybe even better than his younger sister.

18

I thought the role of an older brother was to comfort, protect, and defend his younger sister. That's what I witnessed on TV, in our neighborhood, and at school. My relationship with Jimmy was the opposite.

"Jimmy," I said to him in his mid-fifties, "The staff tells me you're upset. Is that true?"

"They make me mad! They always tell me what I can't eat." I knew this meant he was indulging in donuts, cookies, and soda, sending his sugar level too high.

"Jimmy," I say calmly, attempting to reduce his agitation, "All we want is for you to be healthy. Please follow the rules, okay?"

"I don't like it here. I want to live with Dad."

"You know that's not possible. You have a nice apartment and plenty of activity where you are. Try to make the best of it." It would take a few minutes of listening and encouragement to settle him down. Then I'd redirect him by asking about Philadelphia sports.

Jimmy was smiling and showing behavioral improvements within two months of taking Prozac. I had typed up a set of "Daily Reminders" and posted them on his door. Some included: Smile, Be Polite (cover your mouth when sneezing or yawning, don't burp or fart in public), Use a Calm Voice (do not curse or shout, use words to express your feelings), Follow Directions of Staff Members. "I'll try," he said.

However, in another three months, the verbal outbursts returned. Jimmy was disrespectful and argumentative with the social workers. He complained about the food and didn't participate in group activities. He refused to leave his room during a fire drill. He'd disappear in the middle of the night. He talked about hurting himself.

One day he said, "I want to cut my legs off." Finally, the social worker called me when Jimmy said he planned to jump off the balcony.

After thirty-six hours in the emergency room of the county medical center, Jimmy was transferred to a state psychiatric hospital fifty miles from his apartment. I researched the hospital, located in an urban area known for its violence. I obsessed about his personal safety. Jimmy had never been in a racially diverse environment and I worried about his ability to adapt, particularly in his fragile condition. Would he be scared in those strange surroundings? Would he get the treatment he needed? Would a hospital worker take advantage of him? I made multiple calls to the social workers trying to discern his status.

I had to wait another twelve hours until I could talk to Jimmy. With so much protocol in the facility, I strove to remain even-tempered to whoever answered the phone. One administrator finally connected me to my brother.

"Jimmy, what happened?"

"Ahh . . ." I could hear the exasperation in his voice. "I got problems back at the apartment."

"What do you mean?"

"I didn't like the food. I screamed at myself. I don't have any friends." His tone was low and resigned. My heart ached. I felt helpless. Jimmy assumed the tone of whoever spoke to him, so I did my best to sound positive.

"Jimmy, I love you and your whole family loves you. We want you to get better."

"Uh . . ." Big sighs came from the other end of the line. This was the most difficult conversation I'd ever had with Jimmy—harder than telling him Mom had died. The invisible elastic band stretched between the miles separating us.

"Jimmy, what are you feeling?"

"I don't think you would like it here, Joyce." This time he sounded like a protective big brother.

"No?"

"No. It's different."

"How do you mean different?"

"A lot of workers here speak Spanish. I can't understand them. I want to be back at my apartment."

"Jimmy, you have to let the doctors and nurses help you get better first. Then you can go home."

"Yeah." Big exhalation. "A couple of doctors are trying to help me."

"Good, Jimmy. Cooperate with them and you'll be home soon."

"They took my wallet. I don't have any underwear or clothes." I pictured him at the nurse's station, shifting foot to foot, left to right. He does that when he's anxious or unsure.

"The staff will bring you your clothes tomorrow. I'll call you tomorrow, okay? I love you, Jimmy."

"Uh-kay. Bye."

I hung up and bent my head to my knees in anguish. I felt

like my lungs were collapsing and I had no oxygen left in me. All I kept thinking about was my poor, dear, brave brother. I stared at the clock through the tears and resolved to count the days and hours until he got home.

19

I admire people who remain calm in a crisis and know how to solve problems. In my adult life, a few managers inspired me with their leadership and level-headedness during challenging business times such as layoffs and budget cuts. As a young girl, I was inspired by Julie Andrews's character Maria in *The Sound of Music* because she wasn't afraid to speak up and take risks. In high school, many teachers served as role models. They demonstrated how to deal with conflict. I'd observe them and develop confidence to emulate their behaviors when faced with conflict of my own.

My eleventh grade English teacher had the reputation for being prim and no-nonsense. She established her standards from day one and you had to work hard to earn an A. "By the end of the school year, each of you will become a Turner Product," she informed us on the first day, with her nose in the air. Students looked at each other with puzzled faces. I was captivated.

"When you're in my classroom, you're mine," said Mrs. Turner. "You're only on loan to your parents." She continued by explaining how we got to live at home for a mere eighteen years before breaking out into the world on our own, "so you better make something of yourselves." She expected well-spoken, well-read students exiting her classroom in June. Being a Turner Product also meant we'd write well, become critical thinkers, converse intelligently, and have read classic works of literature like *The House of Seven Gables*, *Walden*, and *Jane Eyre*.

I was spellbound. Probably as much as Mom was at West Catholic reciting poetry and the opening paragraph to *Treasure Island* which she prided herself doing at home occasionally. Mom would have been intoxicated sitting in Mrs. Turner's classroom. Although they shared a love of literature, their personal styles differed.

Mrs. Turner's ultra-conservative appearance matched her manner. Pearl earrings peeked out under her soft, wavy brown hair. She owned a collection of brooches and would pin one to the collar of a high-waist suit jacket. When she didn't wear a jacket, she'd drape a cardigan over her shoulders. She'd tilt her head, purse her lips, and turn up one corner of her mouth as if she knew a secret about you. She spoke with the eloquence of a Shakespearian actor and never raised her voice. Instead, she modulated it with a hypnotic cadence even when criticizing us or teaching manners.

"Close your mouth," she'd say coolly to a boy yawning in the back row. "I don't care to see your uvula." Her slow-forming smile appeared at every opportunity to introduce a new vocabulary word. If someone gave her a smart-aleck response, she'd reply with unforgettable poise, "Mr. Lewis, you insipid snip." Though brief and unique in her critical remarks, we learned to rise to her standards. Mrs. Turner held my attention unlike any other teacher. She wielded power and influence with a calm demeanor, unlike the macho images on TV. She and Mom telegraphed that they believed in me. They saw potential and expected more of me than I expected of myself.

In the early 1970s era of free love and the peace movement, what really stuck with me was Mrs. Turner's lesson on transcendentalism. I'll never forget the way she explained self-reliance. Instead of her usual perfect script penmanship, she wrote the word in large block letters on the blackboard. We'd read Ralph Waldo Emerson's famous essay on the topic and it fascinated me. His words "*Trust thyself*" meant not necessarily relying on my parents for every decision or adopting their thinking as my own. Emerson gave me permission "*To believe your own thought.*" I could acknowledge my thoughts as valid and valuable. So I set a goal to become self-reliant. Without realizing it, I started to break away from automatically agreeing with my parents' and friends' opinions to form my own ideologies.

One winter day Mrs. Turner summoned me at the end of class. I couldn't imagine what she might want to say to me privately. Standing at her desk, I could smell the clean powdery scent of make-up on her flawless complexion.

"Joyce, very soon you'll be graduating," she said, aligning a stack of papers. "You should become acquainted with a university library and begin researching and writing like a college student now. Ask your parents if they will take you to Villanova's library. I will write a note to their librarian requesting they give you access."

I was speechless. Even then, I knew this was a pivotal point in my life.

"Really? You'd do that?" I had wondered how many other students she'd made this offer to but didn't ask, nor did I tell any classmates. It was my secret and I didn't want anyone else getting the same advantage.

"Of course I will," said Mrs. Turner, giving me her signature smile.

Here was a teacher who imagined bigger things for me than I imagined for myself. A teacher who connected with me, who raised the bar for me. A teacher who believed in me. I accepted the challenge and spent several Sundays that winter in the Villanova University library researching among college students whom I admired. I loved ambling through the woodsy-smelling stacks in solitary bliss. I felt invisible yet safe the way I did running through the bed sheets as a little girl. It comforted me to surround myself with great works of literature and research.

By the end of the school year, I had become a certified Turner Product. More importantly, Mrs. Turner made me feel worthy. My writing had improved. I could name the authors and explain plots of famous American works of fiction. My vocabulary had increased and I'd received a hard earned "A" from Mrs. Turner. I learned more about analytical study and quiet perseverance from Mrs. Turner than I did from any popular, fun-loving teacher. All of that, combined with her confidence in me, pointed me on the path toward self-reliance. Little did I know then how important the trait would become for me to manage crises in adulthood, both with Jimmy and in the business world.

One Sunday morning in the fall of my senior year, Mom nudged my shoulder to wake me. "Come downstairs into the kitchen. Daddy and I want to talk to you," she said. I heard the subtle flap of her slippers as she left the bedroom before having the chance to ask why.

In the twin bed next to me Alison slept, so whatever the matter was it did not include her. My eyes squinted at the horizontal lines of morning light peeking through the venetian blinds of the middle bedroom we shared since Lynne had moved into her own apartment. I put on my robe, shuffled to the bathroom and skipped brushing my teeth before apprehensively treading downstairs.

Turning the corner from the bottom step, I noticed the swinging door between the kitchen and dining room was closed. That door was shut only a few times per year: during holiday dinners, when Mom and Dad prepared their income tax return, or whenever they had a serious conversation. It being neither holiday nor tax season, I knew something important loomed. Still bleary-eyed, I pushed open the creaky door and entered our cozy kitchen, wallpapered in yellow and white plaid to match the harvest gold appliances and cherry cabinets. There I found Mom seated at the round kitchen table, with Dad opposite her, spinning the lazy susan. There was no breakfast food on the table–only their cups of coffee and Mom's ashtray. A smoke signal rose toward the Tiffany lamp.

"So what did you think of East Stroudsburg yesterday?" she asked. The three of us had driven a couple of hours north of Philadelphia to tour the campus of a state college. It rained all day. Most of my time was spent under an umbrella so I didn't see many students and there weren't any classes in session on a Saturday. The only thing I could recall was the small dorm room.

"It's okay, I guess. I liked it," I answered flatly. My idea of college meant living away from my family. After sharing a bedroom with Lynne and Alison all my life, I yearned to leave home, stretch my arms wide, and soak in a place other than Drexel Hill.

"What did you like about it?" Mom inquired.

"I don't know."

"Can you see yourself there?"

"I guess."

A heavy pause filled the room.

"Well, Daddy and I have been talking." She took a drag of her cigarette and waited. "We can't see you there," she said. My mother didn't usually waste time getting to the point. Dad drummed his fingers on the table.

My first thought was: Does this mean I'm not going to college? I didn't want to commute a half hour to Delaware County Community College or West Chester State where many kids from my high school went.

As they watched me absorb Mom's words, Dad piped up.

"It doesn't make sense to send you to the Poconos in the middle of nowhere when we live in suburban Philadelphia, an area full of reputable colleges," he reasoned. "Especially if you're not even excited about it."

I could see his point but I really wanted to live away from home. It would be my chance to break free. Then I wouldn't have responsibility for Jimmy who was attending Elwyn Institute at the time. Established in 1852, Elwyn is one of the country's first schools for children with intellectual disabilities. My mother had written several letters to elected officials to get Jimmy enrolled after graduating from Upper Darby High. For three years, he took a bus to its campus less than ten miles from our home. He learned vocational and life skills from a caring and talented staff. It was a transitional time for Jimmy because his neighborhood friends started moving away and he had to develop new relationships at Elwyn. Jimmy liked it there and was stretching his wings. I wanted to stretch mine, too. However, I didn't know what other options were available.

"Daddy and I don't think going to East Stroudsburg is the right path for you," Mom said, stubbing out her cigarette. "Let's visit some other colleges closer to home. It's a beautiful sunny morning. Go get dressed and we'll make a day of it. We can start with St. Joseph's and then drive down Lancaster Pike and stop at Villanova. Daddy's driven you to their library already, right?"

"Yes."

"We'll look at Bryn Mawr, Rosemont, and Immaculata, too."

I'd heard of those schools but never gave them any consideration.

"What about Temple?" I asked. "They have a respected journalism department."

"You're not going to Temple," Dad said cutting the air with a swift short motion of his flat hand. "It's in a bad section of the city and I'm not letting you go somewhere that's not safe. Forget about Temple."

"Go put on something nice. Not jeans." Mom said as she rose and carried her coffee cup and ashtray to the sink. "Let's get an early start. We have a lot to see."

I slowly got up from my chair and pushed the swinging door into the dining room. My head swam with confusion and excitement as I shuffled back upstairs. What was happening? I sensed a seismic shift in my relationship with my parents. Something positive but unclear was on the horizon. Was I really qualified for a more competitive college or university? My mother surprised me by thinking so.

Mom had desperately wanted to go to college and study literature but it wasn't feasible for a milkman's daughter in the 1940s. Like many of their generation, my grandparents assumed Mom would work a few years before marrying and raising a family. Grandmom did offer to come up with the six hundred dollars to send Mom to nursing school. Mom wasn't interested in hospital work so she became a secretary before settling down into marriage and motherhood. I detected a tinge of resentment whenever she talked about her lost opportunity. However, she became heartened when my turn came to apply to college. Mom would experience higher education through me.

Little conversation took place during the twenty-minute drive to the first campus visit. I didn't get a vibe at St. Joe's so we headed to Lancaster Pike, the main artery crossing virtually every town on the Main Line. The Main Line was and still is a beautiful and affluent region of real estate stretching about twenty miles from Philadelphia to Paoli. Mom occasionally shopped in Wynnewood and Ardmore so I was familiar with those towns, but never imagined myself becoming part of their landscape. Bryn Mawr College was situated in the bucolic town of its namesake, but I had no intention of attending an all-girls school. Despite their rolling hills and pastoral beauty, that ruled out Rosemont and Immaculata, too. Not to mention the fact that I didn't want to be around nuns. I'd had enough of them at St. Bernadette's.

Cruising up the hill from the hamlet of Rosemont to Villanova, my heartbeat quickened. The sun shone, a sharp contrast from the dreariness of the prior day in the Poconos. The cerulean sky beckoned us forward and I remembered the route when Dad drove me there at Mrs. Turner's recommendation. The first time Dad chauffeured me to the Falvey Memorial Library, he proudly informed me that he was on the construction crew who built the stately edifice.

"There's more reinforced steel in the library than in any of the other buildings on campus. You know why?"

"No. Why, Dad?"

"To support all the books. Books are heavy, you know."

As we approached the college, I scooted to the edge of my seat and rolled down the window to get a closer look at the campus. Although I had been there several times before, now I was seeing it in a new light. The cool air brushed my face and I sensed the world extending its arms wide open around me. A rush of energy propelled me forward and I couldn't stop smiling. My excitement grew as I marveled at the stone academic buildings and Gothic architecture. I stared enviously at the students sauntering across manicured grounds and imagined myself doing the same. Until then, I had considered Villanova far beyond my academic reach. Then, on that Sunday drive, I reconsidered if indeed it might be the right place for me. Why not? Mom turned around from the front seat with a grin and raised eyebrows. I caught Dad's twinkling glance in the rear-view mirror.

The next day, without an appointment, Mom and I headed directly to the admissions office in Tolentine Hall where I was interviewed. When the distinguished female interviewer named Mrs. Burns asked me about my teachers, I told her how Mrs. Turner challenged me and that I'd been using the Villanova library while in high school. I said that although I didn't do well in math and hadn't a career choice in mind at the time, I wanted to study in the College of Liberal Arts. I did my best to convince her I'd find my calling at Villanova even though I had never opened the course catalog.

When Mrs. Burns escorted me back to the reception area after our fifteen-minute chat, she nodded to Mom with a gentle, telling smile. Mom and I strolled through the leafy campus of diagonal walking paths after the interview. Its energy was palpable and every fiber of my body danced. After that visit, all I could think about was Villanova. Mom was equally excited but careful not to show overconfidence or doubt.

At home that night, Dad brought me back down to earth as the three of us sat around the kitchen table again.

"All we can afford is a state college," he said. "However, Mommy and I don't want you to miss out on an opportunity like Villanova. We saw how happy you were there when we visited. If you go to Villanova, you won't have the full college experience of living away, but you'll get a better quality education." He paused. I knew this was an important talk Dad was having with me and never lost eye contact with him. "You'll have to work part-time through college and take out student loans. That's not so bad. Think of the other kids at Upper Darby High School who plan to work instead of go to college. They'll have car loans and the car will be worth nothing in two years. In fact, as soon as they drive the car out of the dealership, it loses value." He chose his words deliberately and spoke emphatically. "You get out of college what you put into it. When you graduate, you'll have an education no one can ever take away from you. Your education will only increase in value."

That was the best advice Mom and Dad ever gave me. They convinced me I was worthy of more. The potential of attending a reputable school like Villanova eclipsed any disappointment I had about being a commuter and still living at home.

The day after my interview at Villanova I sought out my guidance counselor.

"Mrs. Crowley, I'm applying to Villanova."

"Oh, that's awfully steep for you," she replied shaking her head side to side, chin down.

Heat rose to my cheeks. This woman knew nothing about me. All she cared about were the straight-A, honor society students.

"I went there yesterday and had an interview."

"You did?"

"Yes, and I think it went really well," I said with newfound confidence.

"Well, don't get your hopes up."

She was really irritating me but I had fight inside me.

"Mrs. Crowley, did you know I've used the Villanova library several times already? Mrs. Turner encouraged me and I've done some of my classwork there."

"That may be but you should apply to other schools," she said sifting through papers on her desk. "How about Lycoming College?" she said, handing me a brochure. "That's where my daughter goes."

I refused to be dissuaded. My mother believed in me and so did Mrs. Turner. I fixed my gaze on Mrs. Crowley and said to myself: *Listen to me, you old coot. I'm going to get in, you'll see. Go ahead and take credit for the honor society overachievers. I'm going to write a fantastic college essay and I'll get admitted to Villanova with or without your help.*

"I'm not interested in Lycoming," I said placing the brochure on her desk. "Please send my transcript to Villanova." I pivoted and walked away thinking: *Watch me fly.*

A few days later I drove to Uncle Louie's messy real estate office to get the paper application notarized. Uncle Louie wasn't really an uncle, but I'd always called him that. He was brilliant, cynical, and sharp-tongued. When he arrived at our house with his wife to play bridge with Mom and Dad, he'd march into our kitchen and hike up his pants around his rotund build, wasting no time getting down to the business of playing cards. His gravelly voice and hands never stopped. You could hear him from any room of the house telling stories about his four boys or the latest developments in the real estate market. Coincidentally, Uncle Louie had graduated from Villanova and so did two of his sons. I was prepared for him to be gruff. Seated in the wooden swivel chair at his messy desk, he grabbed the forms from my hand.

"Why are you applying to Villanova?" he snapped. "You're a girl. West Chester State is good enough for you. That's where my two daughters went." I wondered if his daughters wanted to go elsewhere and whether he deprived them of their dreams.

Uncle Louie's razor-sharp eyes cut right through me. I'd never seen this side of him. I'd only known him as the guy who talked fast and made Mom and Dad laugh while playing bridge. He studied me, waiting for a reply. For what seemed like an hour, I stood there wondering if he was serious or joking. He was serious all right. I held my ground and refused to be intimidated.

"Because that's where I want to go."

He stared at me for another moment then shook his head.

"I'll notarize this," he said opening the desk drawer to retrieve his seal. "But tell your parents I think it's a waste of time and money."

"Thank you, Uncle Louie." I gingerly took the application from him, hoping he wouldn't snap it back. Then I swiftly left his office before he had the chance to bark again. He never got up from his seat.

A fat envelope arrived in the mail several weeks later. I brought my fist to my mouth in anticipation of the good news before reading the first word, *Congratulations!* Take that, Mrs. Crowley. Ha-ha, Uncle Louie.

Mom and Dad were proud and relieved especially because,

as I discovered years later, they never wanted me to live away at college in the first place. I'm certain they wanted the best quality education for me first and foremost, but an additional benefit to me living at home was the fact that I'd still be around to help out with Jimmy. I don't think they'd ever admit it but I've sensed it to be true. Although their rationale about the plethora of colleges near our home was valid, I'm sure the idea of losing the dutiful, compliant child and paying boarding costs were situations they preferred to avoid.

They fixed up the finished side of the basement as my study room, the scene of the famous dart throw and place where Jimmy and I performed his exercises. Mom and Dad bought a red shag area rug to cover the cold tile floor and encouraged me to decorate the rest of the space as I pleased. I positioned the old, drop-leaf kitchen table perpendicular to Grandpop's antique mahogany desk for more workspace. That little retreat made up for not being in a dorm. I loved the solitude it provided me.

While I was in my freshman and sophomore years at Villanova, Jimmy continued his last two of three years at Elwyn. We both commuted on the bus to the 69th Street Terminal and then transferred in different directions. Jimmy would return home ready to shower and relax. I'd return home ready to study. Several times, I headed down the basement with my canvas book bag only to find Jimmy there with a few buddies playing table hockey. He'd invaded my space. I never told him to get out nor did I complain to Mom or Dad, because even though it was repurposed as my study room, it was still the family basement. I couldn't study in the bedroom I shared with my sisters, so I got in the car, drove around the neighborhood and stewed.

It didn't make sense to argue with Jimmy. I was born to resolve conflict, not create it. That was my job at home as the middle child and it would become an essential career skill. I developed confidence and fortitude because two strong, smart women—my mother and Mrs. Turner—believed in me.

My parents celebrate Jimmy's graduation from Elwyn
Media, Pennsylvania
1977

20

In the winter of my sophomore year I found myself invading Jimmy's space. Mom had quarantined me in his bedroom with mononucleosis. She insisted I stay there for the better part of a month while Jimmy bunked with Lynne and Alison in the girls' room. This wasn't the way I had hoped to get my own room. I protested internally because, let's face it, what sister wanted to be near her brother's cooties? Worse, what sister wanted her brother bringing his cooties into her bed?

Jimmy never complained about involuntarily surrendering his room. He never resented me nor did he ask when he could return to his own bed.

"Can I come in?" he knocked softly on the door.

"Of course, Jimmy. It's your room," I murmured.

He rummaged through his drawers and left with his clothes, notebook, and pencils. He had a habit of carrying around a notebook and sharpened pencils, always prepared to document daily observations or numbers of anything: sports scores, money figures, weather temps. He was so gentle and kind. I'd have been ticked off if I had to give up my own bedroom.

There was, however, one perk to having mononucleosis.

I heard the car door slam in the driveway. Mom led the way upstairs for our handsome family doctor who made a house call to see me. Trim and fit, he entered the bedroom tilting forward, his shoulders leading the way as he carried a black medical bag. He must have been in his early thirties–attractive in a way no college guy could be at the time.

Dr. Braunfeld smiled hello. There I lay prone–a sallow, unshowered lump of anemic early womanhood in my brother's bed. As the doctor examined me, I examined him. His closely cropped wavy brown hair and round, rimless eyeglasses gave him an air of sophistication and intellect. His perfect white teeth glistened like piano keys. His unblemished, tanned skin suggested a recent Florida vacation. He raised the stethoscope to his ears above a crisp, laundered collar. When he bent down close, his musk after-shave made me dizzy with desire. Then he asked me to lower the bed sheet and raise my nightgown so he could feel my spleen and liver. His warm, slender hands massaged my abdomen and I didn't want him to stop.

"Her temperature is still over 100," said my mother from the doorway.

"Yes," he answered. "Drink plenty of fluids," he said to me, closing his medical bag.

"Okay, doctor."

"And get your rest."

"When can I go back to school?"

"This will last a few weeks. Get in touch with your professors and let them know you won't be there."

Make-up work. That and my sickly complexion were all I could think of. I feared falling behind in my courses and missing out on social activities.

Jimmy's room measured ten feet by twelve feet. His dresser, made of nondescript wood with a gray-wash color, matched the nightstand. He had a pancake of a pillow. The heating vent on the wall opposite the bed connected to the kitchen vent directly below, precisely where my mother sat at the kitchen table by the wall phone. Her morning routine meant sitting in that corner spot. She drank coffee, smoked cigarettes, and completed the daily crossword puzzle, Jumble and Cryptogram before embarking on anything else. Sometimes I could hear her telephone conversations.

"Joyce is so sick," she said. "The doctor wants to put her in the hospital. I don't know when she's going to get better." Mom had been bringing me trays with the standard hospice fare: chicken broth, apple juice and Jell-O. I barely touched the food. My illness interrupted her routine. I encouraged her to go about her day and play tennis, that I'd be okay. One morning, alone and yearning for a cup of tea, I dragged myself out of bed and headed to the stairs. My legs buckled and I fell halfway down. I hadn't realized how dehydrated and weak I'd become.

The fatigue overwhelmed me. My head hurt and it felt as heavy as a medicine ball. My neck was as thick as a linebacker's and my narrow face drooped longer and sadder. Brown crescent moons deepened under my eyes and the pinkness vanished from my cheeks. My greasy hair and body smelled like a locker room. Baby cacti sprouted on my legs and my hairy armpits were matted and sticky. Naturally, Mom complied with the doctor's order to allow me sponge baths instead of a shower. She changed the bed sheets regularly and wiped down the room, but I still felt dirty and gross. I begged her to allow me to wash my hair and always received a stern "No." After all her lectures about cleanliness, it surprised me that she refused to ignore the doctor's rules on that matter.

At the foot of Jimmy's bed, Farrah beamed as if to say "You wish you looked like me, don't you?" The iconic poster of Farrah

Fawcett in her red bathing suit was taped to Jimmy's bedroom wall. There beamed Farrah, the Seventies bombshell. I envied her rosy, smooth skin and shiny, blonde hair cascading in waves down her shoulders. My hair hung straight and limp, brown and boring. Farrah's toothy Pepsodent smile sparkled. I had a gummy smile. Farrah's Lycra swimsuit barely contained her voluptuous chest. Me, barely a B cup. She had curves. I didn't. I was a nineteen-year-old college sophomore who wanted to look like Farrah, not at her. When I woke up, Farrah was still there. When I dozed off, she was the last thing I saw. And I'm certain she stared at me while I slept.

Truthfully, I aspired to look like Jaclyn Smith, whom I considered the prettiest of the three *Charlie's Angels*, the hit television series of the late 1970s. Jimmy dubbed Lynne, Alison, and me his angels. He called Lynne, Nin, who was more the Kate Jackson leader type. When he called Alison, he dropped the "i" and it came out Al-son. Although a brunette, she was more the Farrah Fawcett type with big wavy hair and lots of sex appeal. Being the quiet one, I was closer to Jaclyn Smith. I wondered if Jimmy really thought we looked like them or if he simply wished we did. Either way, we were flattered by the comparison.

Jimmy's bed faced the dresser with a mirror on top of it. When I sat up in bed, an unrecognizable face reflected back at me, swollen and yellowish. To my left, the poster of supermodel Cheryl Tiegs covered a large part of the wall. She wore a pink bikini with less fabric than a dinner napkin. Her blonde hair flowed and her skin glowed. Posed with her right hand on her hip and her left hand on her firm thigh, a perfect slope matched the tautness of her abs. Her manicured fingernails were polished a subtle pinkish white. (Maybe I could at least have her fingernails.) Her eyes twinkled, and she radiated a confident smile with perfectly straight white teeth. I heard her say, "Yes, I know I'm pretty and you're not."

No one thought to remove the posters. I was in Jimmy's room. I'd rather have stared at the poster of Mark Spitz that Lynne taped next to her bed in our room. He wore a patriotic Speedo swimsuit with seven Olympic gold medals draped over his dark muscular chest.

It hurt my eyes to watch TV or read so I listened to the radio. I learned all the songs on Fleetwood Mac's *Rumours* album that February of 1977. Get well cards and letters decorated the dresser. I gazed longingly at the beautiful gold box of chocolate-covered caramel lace that Aunt Dolores sent me, wishing for my appetite to return.

One night into the second week of my quarantine, Mom and Dad came home and entered the makeshift infirmary together.

"Here, Joyce. We bought you a new pillow," Mom said, pulling it from the Sears shopping bag. That was one of the most memorable gifts I ever received and such a surprise because I hadn't asked for it. As I lay my head on the soft cloud, the achiness subsided.

"Thank you! Thank you!" I said between aahs. I saw the surprise in their faces. They hadn't realized a simple gesture could bring me immense relief.

Finally, after three weeks in bed, I called for Alison.

"Will you ask Mom if I can have a Tastykake?" When Alison relayed my request for the sweet confection famous in the Philadelphia area, Mom rushed up the stairs.

"You want Tastykake, Joyce?" Mom asked clasping her hands.

"Can I have Butterscotch Krimpets?" I answered feebly.

Mom ran into the hallway and yelled downstairs to Dad.

"Joyce wants Tastykake! Hurry, Babe! Go to V&B and buy them. She must be getting better."

Carefully, I peeled away the wax paper wrapper so as not to leave any of the yummy butterscotch frosting on it. I slowly sunk my teeth into the first bite. My taste buds danced. The creamy frosting coated the inside of my mouth into a sugary wonderland. The moist sponge cake was a buttery cushion on my teeth and tongue. *Ahhh.* I'd been cured.

The next day, Jimmy got his room back and I returned to my own bed. The rosy color returned to my cheeks. At least I had that in common with Farrah and Cheryl.

21

Jimmy graduated Elwyn after my sophomore year at Villanova. While I still commuted to college, he boarded a bus at the same corner and transferred to a second one that took him in the other direction to the hamlet of Swarthmore. The staff at Elwyn helped him begin a new chapter of working full-time as a custodian at an apartment complex. He stunk of sweat and swill when he arrived home which is probably why no one ever bothered him. By dinnertime, he'd showered and usually had a story to tell.

"Guess what?" he said between bites of meat loaf.

"What, Jimmy?" Mom asked.

"I found a diamond ring today." That's how Jimmy told a story. He'd get right to the point. No build-up. He knew how to attract our attention. Sometimes he'd interject by raising his voice and waving his hands if he couldn't contribute or find interest in another conversation going on in the room.

"You did? What happened, Jimmy?"

"This lady. This lady . . ."

"Finish chewing, Jimmy."

"This lady. This lady . . ." The volume of his voice increased with excitement. His neck slightly bulged out, then in. "She was crying. She lost her ring. She couldn't find it. She said maybe it fell in the trash." He paused, baiting us.

"Then what happened, Jimmy?"

He swallowed hard before speaking again.

"She . . . she . . . she asked me, would I look in the trashcan for her ring."

"In the trash can? You went through all the trash cans, Jimmy?" asked Mom.

"Yes. Yes, I did. I looked in the trashcans inside first. Then I went outside and I found her ring in the Dumpster."

He swirled a piece of meat loaf in brown gravy and took another bite. We held our forks waiting for the rest of the story.

"What kind of ring was it Jimmy?"

"Gold . . . with a big diamond. She was happy. I gave it to her. She gave me a hug."

Mom exhaled with pride and said, "Oh Jimmy. You're such a good boy." Mom used this phrase countless times through the years, even well into his adulthood.

"Yes," he said and took a swig of milk. He nodded to himself in agreement. His lips jutted out–a distinctive habit.

We sighed, all of us thinking the same thing: how honest Jimmy was.

When the owner of the apartment complex found out, he informed Dad that Jimmy had a job for life. Mom and Dad were relieved until a few years later when the owner sold out to a developer who converted the apartments to condominiums and fired the entire staff.

During my college years I made myself less available at home and liked it, even as a commuter. However, the pull of family responsibility continued. At first, I'd finish my classes and rush home to find housework Mom had left. She'd taken up tennis and was finally doing something for herself and making new friends. I saw Mom in a new light.

Only when I reached midlife myself did I realize how important it was for Mom to have an outlet. In addition to the obvious health benefits, tennis widened her social circle, gave her confidence and something else to talk about. She smiled more and eagerly recounted her great shots to Dad when he came home from work.

I remember feeling obligated to finish all the chores before she arrived home from the tennis club. Before I sat down to study, I'd pick up the clothes, put away the dishes, pass the vacuum, and even make Mom's bed sometimes. When she noticed what I'd done, she came to expect it of me because Alison was still in high school and Lynne worked full-time. We certainly didn't have the means to hire a housekeeper. I became increasingly peeved and bitter toward Mom for expecting me to perform what I considered her job. Why couldn't I allow myself to have a pleasant time on campus? Why did I feel so obligated to rush home after classes to do housekeeping?

After a while, I wised up by staying on campus after classes and using the library more often. I even got a part-time job there. One day Mom confronted me when I came home minutes before dinner.

"Where were you?" she asked with her hands on her hips, still dressed in a tennis skirt.

"At school."

"All day?"

"Yes." I knew where this was going.

"I came home and the house was still a mess."

"Well, I had to study in the library." I'd scored an understated victory and we both knew it. She could no longer rely on me to tidy up the house while she played tennis.

When I wasn't on campus, I also worked part-time at the shiny new Bamberger's department store selling vacuum cleaners, irons, and those new appliances called food processors. Even there, I was assigned to the Domestics department instead of Junior Fashion. Still, I loved that job and worked as many hours as I could. I felt a sense of accomplishment cashing my paycheck, most of which went to school supplies, public transportation, and social events. Still, I found it difficult to leave the house for anything other than work or school. One Saturday night, I came downstairs feeling curvy and confident in new Levi's jeans.

"I'm going to the cabaret in Ardmore with the girls," I announced.

"Be safe," Dad said turning his gaze from the TV.

"Why don't you take Jimmy with you?" Mom said while leafing through a magazine from the couch.

Stab me with guilt. I'd finally befriended a fun group of girls and now Mom wanted me to bring Jimmy along. My face fell and the excitement I'd built for the evening vanished. Here I was ready to go, Jimmy was upstairs in his room seemingly content, and she expected me to get him dressed up and say "Let's go dancing."

My mother hoped he'd assimilate with my friends now that he had matured somewhat. Also, she needed a break and desired a wider social circle for her son.

My shoulders slumped. Another wet blanket.

"I have to leave now Mom or I'll be late," I said from the edge of the living room.

"It would be nice if you'd take him out with you sometime," she said with arched eyebrows. She licked a finger to turn the page without looking at me.

"Unh," I sighed, feeling the weight of Mom's responsibility shift to me. I refused to debate the issue. I knew Jimmy was content to watch the Flyers hockey game in his room and I wasn't going to interrupt him because Mom thought it was a good idea.

I left the house alone and felt pangs of guilt for the rest of the night. I went to the cabaret and tried to get into a happy, dance mood but couldn't. I kept thinking about what Mom said and wondering how things would have transpired if Jimmy had been with me. Part of me wanted nothing to do with him and another part wanted to bring him along. I imagined maybe, just maybe, he'd fit in with college kids his age in a setting like that. I also knew people would show kindness out of pity. I couldn't handle that. I feared Jimmy would be completely ignored, mocked, or shown disingenuous attention. He was so gullible. Either way, I'd be babysitting and constantly on alert for someone waiting to take advantage of him. I'd have to monitor his beer consumption and make sure he didn't embarrass himself or me by burping out loud. I wanted to relax and hang out with my college friends without responsibility. I tried that night but Jimmy was never far from my mind. I returned home, passed his room, heard him grinding his teeth, and felt yet another pang of guilt.

A mother can only be as happy as her unhappiest child. I witnessed this in Mom. However I didn't see Jimmy as unhappy in his early years. Although needy, he had friends, played and watched sports, went swimming and bicycling, and received plenty of attention from people when he spoke.

Still, Mom's worry about Jimmy's daily activities and his future permeated our family life because he was vulnerable and gullible. At too young an age, I adopted the maternal worry trait through osmosis and it bonded me to Mom. As I'd come to learn much later, all mothers worry, particularly for the child who shows weakness of any kind. This became apparent to me when my daughters began school. I saw them and their classmates with varying social needs and learning styles. That provided a deeper level of understanding and acceptance for me as a parent. Of course, that didn't prevent me from constantly worrying—for my own children and still for Jimmy as an adult.

22

I tried to connect with my mother over our love of reading.

"I want to read you a poem we discussed in my British Lit class today," I said, bringing my anthology to the dinner table after the dishes were cleared. "It's called 'The Lake Isle of Innisfree' by William Butler Yeats." Mom shifted in her seat to pay close attention while I read every word with clarity and purpose. Dad sat passively. "It's beautiful, isn't it?" I asked lifting my head from the book.

"What's it mean?" Dad asked.

"It's about his search for peace. Like Henry David Thoreau at Walden Pond. I'd love to go to a place like that." Only in my subconscious did I know that I searched for a peaceful place where I could be free and responsible for no one but myself.

"I know all about Thoreau and Emerson," Mom said, tapping ashes into the ashtray, "but I'm not interested in the Irish poets." She pushed her chair back and said, "Let me read you something that I love." She went to the next room, opened her desk, and retrieved a wrinkled paper. She sat down again, this time pulling the chair closer to me so that we were shoulder to shoulder and I could see the words. Mom read with clarity, "Go placidly amid the noise and haste and remember what peace there may be in silence." She continued slowly reading the rest of the beautiful essay, "*Desiderata*," by Max Ehrmann. I've never forgotten how Mom used her pointer finger under each word nor have I forgotten the message of peace in that timeless essay and have always been grateful to my mother for sharing it with me.

Still, it became clear that Mom was jealous and wanted to compete with me. I lacked the confidence to have an intellectual debate with her because I viewed Mom as the person who took care of the family, paid the bills, cleaned the house, and did the laundry. I didn't see her as a lover of literature until years later. Furthermore, I naively assumed whatever critique or interpretation the English professor gave was the correct and only one.

At the dinner table, Mom would admonish me if I used a new vocabulary word in the wrong context. She'd cite an author or classic piece of literature and wait to see if I knew as much as she did. I didn't know how to respond. She'd often tell Lynne or me to "Go get the encyclopedia" to find the answer to a question. She'd have made a great copy editor, so eager to find and correct grammatical errors. If she'd been willing to learn the computer, I'm convinced she'd have become addicted to it.

Eventually, I stopped sharing class material with Mom and left the academic discussions at school. I felt relieved, and realized that refraining from in-depth conversations with Mom made life easier for me. I also learned to nod my head and say "mm-hmm" to avoid conflict.

Every conversation with Mom was a lesson for my siblings and me. "Pronounce your i-n-g's" she'd demand to us as we rolled our eyes. Besides grammar usage, lecture topics ranged from the correct way to slice celery to how to comport myself in the classroom or on the job. "You should have ..." and "I would have ..." comments deflated me after any pleasurable experience such as a first date or job interview. She repeatedly told me to "be productive" every day. I heard other moms tell their kids to "have fun" but I never heard those words from Mom. Our household was primarily about responsibility, learning, and chores. That's why I didn't see making friends and playing as an option or a priority. I followed Mom's lead and developed a serious personality instead of a playful one. By the time I was born, Mom was in the throes of managing Jimmy's emerging developmental needs. She didn't have the time or inclination to be carefree with me or anyone else.

I wanted to be good enough, smart enough, pretty enough, and accomplished. Yet it never seemed like I could do enough to make my mother proud.

Mom likely felt the same. She resented her mother for forcing her to grow up so quickly. As a little girl, Mom would be dispatched to fetch Grandpop for dinner at the Italian social club where he'd been gambling and drinking. Always the youngest in the class, Mom took the elevated train across town by herself at age twelve to buy her plaid high school uniform. She never felt valued as the youngest of three in the family because she claimed that, in Grandmom's eyes, the sun rose and set on her brother Michael. This handsome and intelligent young man became loud and boisterous after getting hit in the head too many times playing football. For this reason, Grandmom helped him dodge the Army and doted on him. Grandmom never intervened when Michael insisted my mother regularly shine his shoes and contribute part of her weekly salary to the payments on his car even though he never let her drive it.

So Mom retreated to reading, which became a lifelong interest. She'd read whatever she could get her hands on:

poetry, magazines, the World Book Encyclopedia, biographies, gardening manuals. She taped favorite quotes to the inside of the kitchen cabinet doors. She frequently fingered through the oversized Random House dictionary openly displayed on an antique school desk in our living room. She mastered the daily crossword puzzle and seized any occasion to write a beautiful letter to a friend or family member. She had insisted I write a thank you note immediately after receiving a gift—something I've passed on to my own daughters.

By my mid-forties, I couldn't deny the personality traits that matched my mother's. I read passionately, and gladly found any opportunity to teach my daughters the meaning of a new vocabulary word. I tended a large garden in the backyard, kept an antique, flip-top school desk in the living room, copied my mother's recipe cards, and faithfully completed the Sunday crossword puzzle.

23

By my senior year of college, Lynne had moved into her own apartment. Alison and I moved into the middle room and my parents finally got their master bedroom. That meant Jimmy frequently woke me up at night in the adjacent room by grinding his teeth or cheering whenever the Flyers scored. The advantage was having a phone next to my bed. I reached my hand to the wall to answer it early one morning.

"Hello," I mumbled as my eyes adjusted to the sunlight slicing the venetian blinds.

"What are you still doing in bed?" my father bellowed.

"What?" I asked, distracted by the cacophony from Dad's job site in the background. He'd called from the office trailer, something rare.

"I said . . . what are you still doing in bed? You should be up, pounding the pavement by now," he said with a half laugh. "Go out and find a job and don't come home until you have one!" Click.

I cradled the phone in my hand and stared at it for an answer. The clock on my desk read 7:00. Couldn't he at least have let me sleep in for one day? I had graduated college the day before but apparently the celebration of a simple family dinner after commencement exercises was short-lived.

I rolled onto my back and noticed Alison's unmade bed next to mine. She would graduate high school the following month and choose secretarial work instead of college. I crossed my arms over my eyes. How had I plummeted from the euphoria of graduation less than twenty-four hours earlier to the misery of that morning? I contemplated what my fellow graduates were doing. Probably sleeping peacefully with the knowledge of a job in hand. The marketable accounting, nursing, and engineering students received job offers before graduation. Friends who had majored in the sciences were headed to medical school. Liberal Arts students like me had to scramble to find a job on our own.

My friends had more direction in their life than I did–even if it was short-term. Peggy and Carol busily planned their cross-country camping trip with their boyfriends. They bought Dad's old station wagon for their once-in-a-lifetime adventure to see the great U. S. of A. Carefree and optimistic, they decided full-time employment could wait a few months. Melinda prepared for law school. Rita had set her sights on Richmond for graduate school and Paul would be packing for Boston where he, too, enrolled in a graduate program. I couldn't even think about pursuing a master's degree right away because I had loans to pay off and couldn't imagine going further into debt.

What in the world was I going to do with a bachelor's degree in English? All the time spent in classes giddy to be analyzing poetry and I never thought about what to do next. Did I really think Eugene O'Neill and William Blake were the answer? How could I have been so impractical to have not made post-graduate plans?

I had nowhere to go. No car. No job. No money. No boyfriend.

For four years I had reveled in campus life and the job at Bamberger's department store where my manager praised me for selling the most food processors of any member of her staff month after month. Even away from home, I excelled in the domestics department. Would that be my life's work? I reached a point of no escape. No campus to commute. No leafy greens to traverse. No basketball games to cheer. No library where I could hide or study.

Jimmy had gotten a job after graduating from Elwyn. He'd proudly show Mom his paycheck and ask when they could go to the bank to cash it so he could buy another piece of sporting equipment. I was jealous of his purchasing power. His confidence grew while mine deteriorated.

Even Mom had jobs. Dad had convinced her she needed to get out of the house and the extra income would help. Mom found secretarial work at an elite financial services firm. She felt privileged and somewhat entitled to work in the company of PhDs who studied and reported on the economy. Naturally, she soaked up as much information as she could and shared stories at the dinner table about her esteemed co-workers. As much as she liked the job, she stayed less than a year. Long hours of office work tired her. She later landed a part-time job at a bridal salon on the exclusive Main Line. She had fun playing dress-up to the women and daughters from wealthy suburbs–until she complained about her arms being constantly in pain from carrying heavy wedding dresses for hours.

Mom had advised me to drive her car to the town of Bala Cynwyd where many employment agencies were located. I showered, dressed, and donned the only nice outfit I owned: a yellow linen skirt and matching blazer. She told me to submit my resume to one or two firms "for their files." I doubted it would do much good. I didn't even know what type of job to seek. Dear God, I prayed, please don't give me an entry-level secretarial job. When Dad arrived home, he asked for a report. I meekly told him about filling out an application at one recruitment agency in the morning and reading the classified ads in the newspaper in the afternoon, but not finding anything. The rest of my boring day included watching TV, doing laundry, and envying other graduates who were either gainfully employed or traveling.

"What? And you think you're gonna get a job that way?" he asked with a laugh.

I opened my mouth to say something but nothing came out.

"You think you can just sit home and wait for the phone to ring? Like someone is going to call you up and say, 'Hey Joyce, come work for us!' You gotta pound the pavement, my dear." With an encouraging tone, he said, "Let people know who you are. The best jobs are with the big companies because they offer the most benefits and opportunities for advancement. Those companies are in town."

"In town?" I asked apprehensively.

"Yes, in town. Tomorrow, you get dressed up again, take the el into Center City and hand out your resume to as many big companies as you can." I heard optimism in his voice. "Go into the office buildings, find and read the directory in the lobby, and leave your resume with the receptionist at each company. *That's* how you look for a job."

I had never traveled to Philly alone. Dad drove the family into town when we went to the Wanamaker's Christmas light show. As long as I was with him I felt protected, but getting through some of those Philly streets alone with throngs of aggressive strangers scared me. Once I arrived, where would

I go? Who would hire me? I didn't even know what my skills were.

The next day I donned the same yellow suit and boarded a bus at the corner that took me to the 69th Street Terminal where I caught the el to 15th and Market Streets, the center of Philadelphia. Although I'd taken public transportation to college, traveling the el all dressed up felt uncomfortable. The thought of bacteria and germs layered on the seats and metal bars from all the coughing, sneezing, stuffy-nosed passengers disgusted me. I tried not to touch anything with my bare hands. I wanted to be rocking on the P&W (Philadelphia & Western train) on the way to verdant Villanova instead of filthy Philly.

I emerged from the el at the iconic architectural clothespin at the Centre Square building (another one of Dad's jobs) and began my trek. I stayed west of Broad Street and walked the three-by-three-block grid of office towers between 15th and 18th Streets, and across Market, Chestnut, and Walnut Streets. I pushed the revolving doors into and out of every office building. I tried to synchronize my pace with the business people around me but felt out of place. The new landscape was not one I was sure I wanted to be part of: grimy streets, dirty concrete, panhandlers, car fumes, screeching buses, sirens, people shoving and rushing, cab drivers skirting within inches of the curb where my new navy pumps quickly lost their shine.

Maybe a job at State Farm in the suburbs where Lynne worked, I reasoned. Or maybe not. I didn't really like the job I had there the summer before entering Villanova. The head clerk told me I worked too fast and she got mad at me when I took the initiative to fold big stacks of policies on her desk one morning before she arrived. When I left at the end of August, she said to me in a snippy voice, "Why are you going to college, anyway?"

Three interviews and a battery of written tests later I was offered a job as an administrative assistant at a Fortune 500 company. I'd graduated college only to become a glorified secretary but was hardly in a position to decline. Two hundred and twenty-five dollars per week plus benefits was considered a decent deal. I'd be able to make my first loan payment, due in September. A job in the city meant I'd entered the big time.

One summer morning a month after starting my job, I caught sight of a drunken bum who I'd seen before, squatting in the alcove of a storefront. In the corner of my eye, I noticed him pull himself up, unsteady on his feet, and come barreling in my direction. I picked up the pace a few strides ahead of him but not fast enough. He swung from behind and whacked me on the side of my head at my right ear. I stumbled in my summer wedges and tugged my purse but caught myself before splatting to the pavement. My intoxicated attacker swung his arms wildly and blathered incoherently. I regained my balance, hobbled to the corner, crossed the street, and pushed through the revolving door of my office building, still breathless. One of the sales managers from the office saw me disoriented and near tears. He put his arm around me and ushered me to the lobby café where I recounted my attack and tried to make sense of what happened. In my mind I heard Dad's pessimistic voice: "It's a cruel world out there."

After my violent initiation to the world of urban professionals, working in town became infectious and fun. My focus shifted from home and family responsibilities to a real job interacting with college-educated employees who challenged me in new and intellectual ways. Work no longer meant housekeeping or helping Jimmy. I'd assumed a new adult and independent role by taking the el with all the other business people from the suburbs. Like I'd done on the P&W heading to Villanova, I invented biographies of passengers dressed in suits, carrying briefcases, snoozing, or reading the *Wall Street Journal* rendering them faceless. A symphony of rattling, horizontal shifts of the commuter car, clanging metal doors, pounding foot traffic, and turnstile clanks forced me into a new groove. I eagerly anticipated chomping a soft pretzel during my lunch break while sitting on the low brick wall outside the United Engineers building, people-watching and wondering if my future husband walked among the crowds. And I was finally making money. With my first paycheck, I bought a Seiko watch from a jeweler on Walnut Street. My confidence grew. So did my savings account that would enable me to set out on my own eventually.

Another autumn day when dressed in a skirt, blazer, and heels, I strolled down to 17th and Spring Garden Streets. That's where Dad worked as the foreman on the SmithKline building. It was the first time I'd seen him in action on the job and he impressed me. He exuded leadership when introducing me to a few of the guys, then warned me to keep my distance from the dangerous site without a hardhat. I stared at countless grids of green rebar (a steel rod with ridges) that Dad explained was used to reinforce concrete on the high-rise. That night at the dinner table, with a wink of the eye, Dad told me to look out my window at exactly noon the next day.

While standing at my window on the thirtieth floor I detected a large piece of plywood in the distance that Dad's crew had hoisted up the high-rise. On it was a message spray painted in black: *HI JOYCE*. The unique gesture made me feel welcome in the city and truly on my way to a business career. I had found a direction after college and, more importantly, a direction that didn't involve Jimmy.

24

While I worked in downtown Philadelphia, Lynne was on her way to becoming a State Farm agent and Alison found administrative work at a boutique law firm. Jimmy carried his weight too, working various jobs after graduating from Elwyn. Mom and Dad firmly believed he should be a taxpaying citizen and not rely on government handouts.

I desperately wanted to leave home. I felt cramped and stifled and was tired of sharing a bedroom with my sister and the bathroom with the rest of the family. I wanted a tranquil place with elbow room but I had to save enough money first and plan a career path that would provide me the security I needed. I knew if I stayed in Drexel Hill that my parents would continue their reliance on me. I'd wind up driving Jimmy places and feel on call. I might never have a social life much less a boyfriend. So at age twenty-four I told Mom and Dad about a job transfer.

"What do you mean you got a job in New Jersey?" Mom asked, lowering the magazine to her lap and leaning forward from the couch. As if New Jersey was on the other side of the earth.

"It's a promotion, Mom," I said standing at the edge of the living room. "I'm going to be a personnel coordinator. Remember? I've been telling you about this job for a few months."

"Yes, but I didn't think you were serious." She turned to Dad who sat speechless.

"I am serious. And I'm excited, too. I'm moving out," I said and turned toward the stairs leaping two steps at a time up to my bedroom. Although I felt disappointed by Mom's lack of enthusiasm, I wasn't surprised. And yet, I found a private glee in shocking her with the news. My mother knew I was capable of more. After all, she had directed me to Villanova. But she never imagined I'd spread my wings further than Delaware County where she could still easily reach out to me and, more specifically, influence me to her way of living.

My apartment was a two-hour drive away from Mom and Dad's house. I was thrilled to buy Laura Ashley bedding from the Spiegel catalog for my new double bed, a couch, dishes and coffee mugs, bath towels, and a portable black-and-white TV. I took my desk, Grandmom's chair, and a maple chair and dining set Mom found at a garage sale. The apartment was serene and peaceful. No more loud burps from Jimmy or wiping the toilet seat from his spray because he was too lazy to lift it up. No more switching cars in the driveway late at night to line up for the next morning's order of departures by Dad, Lynne, and me. If I wanted a pint of Haagen-Dazs Vanilla Swiss Almond ice cream for dinner, then that's what I ate.

The garden apartment was located near an aunt and her family. My cousins provided companionship for me and they made me laugh. I hadn't known it was okay to laugh inside a home the way they did. They poked fun at each other and themselves. I loved walking into their home and not feeling the tension between Mom and me. I felt free of the burden of Jimmy, free of sharing a room with my sister, free to spread my arms wide open, free to make my own decisions and not check in with anyone.

"I think you've forgotten your family," Mom said during one phone call.

"Mom, give me some credit." She knew how to zing a barb and make me feel lousy. I knew she missed me but I took offense at her remark. She didn't ask about my job or my social life. I wished she could be happy for me but it wasn't her nature to be optimistic. She and Dad missed an extra set of hands and the calm I brought to their home. Dad admitted this to me years later, after Mom died.

It was easier to shrug off her comments in my own apartment. I started building an independent life and an exciting career in the emerging technology field.

"Are you coming home this weekend?" my mother asked on a telephone call.

"I just got back from Boston and next week I have to go to Montreal."

"Oh," she said, telegraphing her disappointment. I heard her take a drag of a cigarette. "I don't understand. Why are you traveling so much?"

While I paced my kitchen, I envisioned her sitting at the kitchen table with her feet up on the chair next to her, puffing away.

"Because in this new job I'm responsible for twelve field offices in the Northeast Region and Canada. I have to meet with employees and managers regularly."

"What for? What do you do when you're there?"

"I'm an employee relations specialist. I solve problems in the workplace."

"Like what?"

I stared out the window at a spray of forsythia, eager to get this difficult phone call over with so I could get some sun.

"Well, right now I'm investigating a sexual harassment case."

"Really? How do you know what to do? Who taught you?"

I laughed in a resigned way. Why did she show confidence in me sometimes yet still underestimate me? "I've learned on the job, Mom."

"Well, I don't know how you do those things. And I don't like the idea of you traveling by yourself. Getting on a plane, renting a car in a strange city, checking into a hotel alone. How do you know where to go? What if something happens? Who would you call?"

"Try not to worry, Mom. I'm becoming an experienced traveler and I'll be home for Easter."

In my late twenties, I surprised Mom again by moving farther away. She thought I'd return to the Philadelphia region from northern New Jersey. So did I. Instead, I eagerly accepted my employer's offer to relocate four hours farther north to Massachusetts.

Mom and I never discussed my career plans. I knew if I told her about a job interview in advance, she could cause me to doubt myself and thereby thwart my goals. Although Mom wanted to see me succeed, she rather I'd done so close by in an office doing administrative work she could relate to. A successful woman in the business world was a novel concept to her. She'd have considered me a success if I had married an ambitious Italian guy from Villanova who would have provided me a comfortable lifestyle while I stayed at home raising our full-blooded Italian children. That was the last thing on my mind. I never pined about weddings and babies like my friends did. I dreamed of being on my own. When I finally called to tell her about moving farther away, any hope she had of her dutiful middle daughter returning to the fold was dashed.

"You're moving farther?" I could hear the sadness in her voice.

"It's a promotion, Mom."

"But I thought you were going to come back home."

"This is what I want, Mom." There wasn't much else to discuss. I'd made my decision without her.

The moment I parked my car under an enormous twin oak tree in front of my apartment in an old mansion on historic Main Street, I instinctively felt at home in the world. Living on the outskirts of Boston enabled me to touch history, tour the homes of famous authors, go to concerts and museums, drive forty minutes to the beach and a couple of hours to the mountains of New Hampshire and Maine to ski.

Still, work came first. I welcomed the challenge and got the job done. My chosen career in human resources meant taking on a role that inherently suited me: working in the background to maximize the talent of others.

"I think you should promote Alexis," I said to Jack, the regional sales manager, from across his desk.

"Hmm," he said, steepling fingers to lips. Jack was a clean-shaven West Point graduate who served in Vietnam. He was well regarded for his leadership and decisiveness yet he took time to evaluate what could be a bold decision. "I spent a long time interviewing her and we really clicked. I know she'd do a great job but I'm not sure how it'll go over."

"Think of this, Jack," I said leaning forward, appealing to his competitive nature, "You'll be the first regional manager to hire the first woman in the country as a district manager." His eyes widened and a slow grin emerged. The following day he extended the offer to Alexis. Within the next year, two more women would be promoted to the same position in other regions.

Working at an avant-garde Fortune 100 company known for their "high output management" gave me tons of confidence. Managers encouraged and rewarded their employees for risk-taking, discipline, and influence. I'd drive home grinning with a tremendous sense of accomplishment. All the discipline and drive I developed at that company and throughout my career would serve me well when I retired from corporate life and assumed more family responsibility for my aging parents and brother.

As I excelled, Jimmy expanded his work experience, too. After his custodial job at Wildman Arms apartments, he worked a short stint at a manufacturing plant where they made clothes hampers. The place burned down but not before some guy conned Jimmy into selling him his golf clubs for five dollars. When Dad got wind of it, he confronted the plant manager who easily identified the culprit and returned Jimmy's clubs.

Then Jimmy got a job at St. Charles Seminary in Wynnewood set amidst a rolling expanse of prime real estate on the Main Line. Jimmy once again boarded the bus to 69th Street and transferred to a second bus out to the leafy suburbs. It took him an hour to get to his custodian job. He had worked part-time for about two years when the priests scheduled him to work an additional measly two-hour shift on Saturdays. Dad arrived early to pick him up on what turned out to be Jimmy's last day of work there. Dad found Jimmy, sweaty dirty, lying on the floor picking off what seemingly amounted to ten years of caked, black grease from the oven.

"You mean to tell me no one else who lives here has ever bothered to clean this old oven?" Dad demanded to the priests sitting at the kitchen table sipping their coffee. "You waited until my son got here so you could make him do this filthy job?"

Dad didn't wait for an answer. He gave Jimmy a hand, pulled him up and said, "Get your coat, Jimmy. We're leaving."

Finally, when Jimmy was in his late twenties, Dad took his son to work with him on the construction site. Up until then, Dad had hesitated because he was afraid Jimmy would get hurt. Dad talked to the business agent at the union who agreed to issue Dad a temporary pass for Jimmy. All Dad had to do was apply for the pass on the first of each month and pay dues for Jimmy even though Jimmy was not a member of the union. By then Jimmy was able to perform gopher work. He got paid the union's going rate.

Dad kept Jimmy on the ground, never up on the floors of the high-rises being erected. Jimmy was in charge of the acetylene torch. His job required him to unwrap it in the morning and wrap it up at night. He'd get the hoses and gauges and roll them, along with the heavy torch, on a rack. This could have been tricky for Jimmy given his clumsiness in the past. But Jimmy was husky and strong and he worked carefully, aware of the safety issues on a construction site. He appreciated having responsibility and being among a group of strong men. He hadn't been among a fraternity since his youth playing hockey and basketball with the neighbors.

Dad paired Jimmy up with one of his best workers, a guy named Herbie Cardenas. Herbie taught Jimmy how to use pliers and wire to tie steel rods together. It was backbreaking work, bending over for literally hours on end. Jimmy never complained. It turned out the two of them made a complementary team. Dad admired how Herbie treated Jimmy like a son.

Jimmy worked with Dad in construction for several years until Dad retired in 1988. Soon afterward Jimmy landed a job collecting carts at Acme Supermarket in Drexeline Shopping Center, a few miles from home. Jimmy liked this job primarily because he got tips from the women shoppers for transferring their grocery bags from shopping carts into car trunks. When he arrived home, he'd quickly empty his pockets–all four pants pockets, and at least two jacket pockets including those on the inside. Sometimes lint would attach to a coin. Occasionally, cookie crumbs or a Tastykake wrapper fell out of his palm. He'd pat himself down before the count. Then he'd start sorting while hunched over the kitchen table. He wouldn't even remove his jacket or baseball cap. Quarters, nickels, and dimes were divided into separate piles. He smoothed out dollar bills with both hands as if first setting eyes on an artistic masterpiece. He usually earned twenty to thirty dollars in tips a day.

One year on the day before Thanksgiving he scored close to seventy-five dollars. He kept a mental tally and knew Mondays were less lucrative than Fridays. Then one of the floor managers heard about Jimmy's regular windfalls. The manager walked outside, ostensibly to chat with Jimmy, and slapped him on the thigh in jest. He remarked about Jimmy's loaded pocket and said Jimmy had to split the tips with him fifty-fifty.

When it comes to money, there's no fooling Jimmy. He keeps track of every coin and dollar bill. A coin sorter sat on top of his bureau for years. He still likes to roll coins in brown wrappers and go to the bank to exchange them for dollar bills. I've sensed he's always stashed cash in secret places. He'll spend money on a magazine or coffee for himself but look the other way when it's time to leave a tip at the diner. If something costs $2.99, he'll fan his wallet open toward me and say, "I only have two ones and a ten," never thinking to break the ten.

When Jimmy reported the new supermarket "rule" to my parents, Dad solved the problem immediately. For the next few days, he drove to the store's parking lot and waited in the car where Jimmy met him out of view of the store entrance. Jimmy emptied his pockets into Dad's cupped hands before the end of the shift. Not long after the manager didn't see tips coming his way, the owner of Acme established a new policy of "no tipping."

"It's not fair! Now I can't get any more tips," Jimmy fumed.

We learned later that some customers complained about pressure to tip. So Jimmy was no longer allowed to put bags in the trunk of a car. Instead, he'd wait by the baskets for the shoppers to pull their cars by the entrance and watch the customers load the bags themselves. On several occasions, women drove away absentmindedly leaving their handbag in the cart. Each time, Jimmy retrieved the forgotten valuables and returned the purses to the manager's office.

Jimmy always followed the rules. When the store owner's wife subsequently tried to give Jimmy a tip, he refused. He didn't want to risk losing his job. He worked at the store several more years but his motivation waned. Still, he showed up on time and rarely missed a day. In fact, he got annoyed when I scheduled my wedding on a Friday night because it meant losing three days' pay due to travel.

Working at a grocery store suited Jimmy. He loved to eat and reveled in the perks of spending his break time ordering deli sandwiches, chomping Oreos and cake, and drinking Sprite by the liter while sitting on the bench outside wearing his orange pinny. He wore eyeglasses full-time now and the storefront activity kept him interested and observant. He secured jobs at two other major grocery chains when he and my parents moved to New Jersey. Once when I visited him, instead of his jacket pocket bulging with coins, he reached in and pulled out a days-old, smashed glazed donut in its wrapper.

25

My career was thriving and I loved my newfound freedom. At twenty-seven, I met Gary on a business trip and fell in love. He showed me how to have fun. He bought me a pair of ice skates and we glided on a frozen lake in the town where we lived in northeastern Massachusetts. He took me to buy my first pairs of skis–downhill and cross-country–and we booked winter getaways at ski resorts throughout New England. We bought new bicycles and toured all of Martha's Vineyard and Nantucket in the summer months. We took Caribbean vacations, went canoeing, dined at new restaurants, and went to concerts and baseball games. We were giddy in love, with responsibility to no one but ourselves. We connected on an intellectual level, too. We'd both had jobs with a reputable company in the groundbreaking field of technology. He taught me to be a better listener and I urged him to show more compassion for less fortunate people.

"Mom, Gary and I are moving in together. We bought a house," I said with equal parts excitement and reservation. I knew she would be less than thrilled.

"You bought a house? Up there?" she asked. Clearly she still held out hope I'd return to the Philly area.

"Yes, we're really excited."

"Can you afford it?"

Sigh.

"Yes, Mom." What she didn't know was that I felt more nervous about the emotional commitment than the financial one. Still, I had to move forward.

"But Joyce," she paused. Here it comes. Another roadblock. "I never heard you say you love Gary."

Did she not want me to be happy? Did she want me to break up with Gary and move back home to find a guy whose last name ended in an "i" or an "o"?

With conviction, I replied, "I tell him, Mom, not you."

Many of my mother's friends and family had moved away and she remained stuck in her routine. Her loneliness and dwindling female companionship never dawned on me because I was too absorbed in my own life. During one conversation after Gary and I returned from a weekend getaway, she baited me.

"You know, your father and I would like to take a little vacation. I've always wanted to go to Charleston, South Carolina."

"Then you should go, Mom."

"How can we? Who will take care of Jimmy?"

"He'll be okay on his own for a few days."

Then she said something that cut like a knife: "For someone who's supposed to be smart, you can be awfully stupid."

It felt like I'd been punched in the gut. My mother had forbidden her children from using that word. Now here she was calling me–the studious child, the college graduate, the successful businesswoman–stupid. I sank onto the couch and cried.

"Can you believe she said that?" I asked Gary.

"I can't understand why any mother would say such a thing," he said, shaking his head.

"What am I supposed to do?" I asked him after the second or third time she said it. "Drop everything, leave my job, and babysit Jimmy?" I lifted my head from my hands and said, "I send gifts and cards. I call her. We visit. It feels like I can never do enough and even when I do, it's still not good enough." I'd be sad for a day or two and redirect myself to my job where I felt competent and appreciated.

Gary and I continued to move forward and, two years after moving in together, I called Mom with the big news.

"Mom, Gary and I are getting married."

Slight pause.

"Well, that's exciting news." I could hear reservation in her voice.

"Wait until you see my diamond ring. It's gorgeous," I said, tilting my hand back and forth to watch the rainbow of colors on the ceiling.

"When are you planning to get married?" Alison had gotten married a month earlier. Mom and Dad sprung for an engagement party and the wedding. Despite lovely celebrations, the stress caused regular screaming matches between Mom and Alison as well as Mom and Dad for months. They argued about the invitation list, flower budget, and increasing costs of what was supposed to be a modest affair.

"Probably next spring."

"That soon? I better call St. Bernadette's right away."

"No, Mom. We're going to have a small ceremony here."

"Where?"

"Here, where we live."

The line went quiet. I doubt she even reached for a cigarette.

"Don't you want to come home to get married?"

"I am home."

A heavy pause followed my terse pronouncement. It came out so quickly. I hadn't meant to hurt her. Yet I never dreamed of a traditional wedding with all the hoopla. Even after attending my friends' and cousins' weddings, I couldn't imagine a spectacle for myself. It wasn't me.

"Mom, you don't have to do anything. I'm going to plan a very simple affair. It'll be family only. All I want is for Daddy to walk me down the aisle. That's it. All you have to do is buy yourself a pretty dress and show up. I'll take care of everything."

Mom was mildly disappointed to not have a hand in planning the wedding, but since I relieved her and Dad of the financial burden, there wasn't much she could say. The next day another call came.

"Your father and I have been talking about your wedding. We understand you want to plan everything yourself but there's one thing we really want to do."

"What?"

"We want to send out formal announcements the day after your ceremony. We're very proud of you, Joyce, and we're happy to welcome Gary into our family. We want to share this momentous news with your aunts and uncles and our friends—all the people who saw you grow up."

"Okay," I happily agreed.

"Yeah," my father piped up from the other extension. "Your mother and I have been going to all your cousins' weddings, showers, and engagement parties for the last fifteen years. We've spent a lot of money. It's your turn to get a gift," he said emphatically.

Two days before the big day, my parents and Jimmy arrived.

"How come you're getting married on a Friday night?" Jimmy asked.

"Because that date worked out the best for us, Jimmy."

"I had to miss three days of work, you know," he said. He wanted to make sure I knew he was sacrificing wages and tip money to attend my wedding.

"I'm sorry Jimmy, but I'm so glad you're here now. We'll have a nice few days together," I said, patting him on the shoulder.

The night before the wedding, I was preparing a cheese tray in the kitchen when Mom called me into the living room. There she had spread out several boxes wrapped in white paper and bows.

"I never got to throw you a shower. Aunt Anna, Mrs. Verdi, and a few others asked me to bring you these," she said, fanning her arms above the presents.

"Oh, Mom, this is so nice."

"Come on," she said, leading me by the elbow. "Sit down and open your gifts from Daddy and me first."

I wore the pearl bracelet on my wedding day and put the Lladro bride and groom porcelain figurine atop our wedding cake. Gary and I bought a dining room set with the money Mom and Dad gave us. Their gifts were a surprise. The quiet pre-wedding celebration with only my family felt natural. I didn't want anything more.

The private and understated ceremony at a New England inn suited me perfectly. Although the type and location wasn't what Mom had expected, she quickly acknowledged the tasteful affair I planned without her. She relaxed and chatted easily during cocktails. When it came time to say goodbye, she and Dad lingered in the lobby waving while I stepped into the elevator with my new husband. The expression on her face told me I'd done well. I saw joy in her eyes and sadness too at the thought of losing me again.

26

Mom timed her calls to me as soon as I walked in the door after a long day of work. I'd be sorting through bills and wanting to get out of my business suit and heels and into sweats to prepare dinner. Of course, she'd probably waited all day to talk to me. Her calls intensified with anger when I became even busier with crying, hungry babies. I heard frustration and depression in my mother's voice. She complained about Dad's quirks, said he was too noisy and breathed too loud. She said she was tired of giving Jimmy the same directions to comb his hair, brush his teeth, and tuck in his shirt. Many times I was forced to cut her short and tell her I'd call back.

One Saturday morning in May I was standing in my bedroom with an armful of laundry listening to her rant about how she was sick and tired of having to constantly remind Jimmy to tuck in his shirt, stop biting his knuckles, and say "excuse me" after burping. Jimmy had matured into his thirties. His issues became more burdensome as our parents aged.

"Babe, pick up the other line," she'd yelled to Dad.

That signaled she had something important to say and wanted me to know Dad was in agreement. There were many "You –" statements: *you don't, you aren't, you never*. Maybe I hadn't called them in a while but I don't think I'd done anything unkind. The volume and intensity of Mom's voice increased and before I knew it, she and Dad were fighting and yelling at each another while trying to make a point to me. Suddenly Dad shouted something I've never forgotten.

"And now there's no one here to take care of us!"

Silence.

I was numb and don't remember what any of us said after that.

I was never supposed to leave Drexel Hill. They knew, even before I knew myself, I'd never return. The call ended and Dad's phrase echoed in my mind for years. It finally dawned on me their plans never included me moving away from home. They'd hoped I'd marry a local Italian boy who'd graduated Villanova instead of an Irish boy from Boston. They expected I'd live in a nearby town, bring my full-blooded Italian children to their house once a week for a gravy dinner, and spend every holiday with them.

I felt confused because whenever we parted from a visit, either at her house or mine, Mom would kiss me and give me a big hug. Then she'd put her hands on my shoulders, smile at me, turn to Gary and say, "My Joycie looks happy. I don't know what you're doing Gary to make her so happy but keep doing it."

Still more phone calls came and she sounded disconsolate. She had developed arthritis and suffered with frequent headaches. She said as a redhead she felt pain more acutely than brunettes or blondes. It shocked me when she started using profane language. I hadn't realized how depressed she was.

"Mom, I don't use that language with you. You can't use it with me," I said firmly. She quieted for a moment before letting out a big sigh.

"I'm so frustrated, Joyce. Okay? I'm sorry." I don't recall my mother apologizing for anything; she was always right. So despite her anger, her apology was a small victory for me.

Living with Jimmy and Dad must have been lonely and overwhelming. Some friends had moved away and she'd stopped playing tennis. Even though she could be brutally direct, she often spoke in parables when trying to convey something. She'd tell a story about one of her friends' children and what they'd accomplished or what exotic family vacation they'd had. She hinted about wanting to go to Italy several times. Most times I'd remain silent and not bite. How was I supposed to coordinate an extended vacation with my young family, Mom, Dad, and Jimmy and lead them around Europe? I hadn't the energy, not to mention the extra vacation time. I needed to use my three weeks of vacation a year for my children's school breaks.

"You're always busy," she said. "In the morning, you're getting the girls ready for school, at night you're fixing dinner and getting them their baths. You don't want me calling you at the office. When am I supposed to talk to you?"

"Mom, it's better if I call you on the weekends when I have more time," I suggested.

"You mean I can't call you during the week? I have to wait for you to call me?"

I could feel her hurt and bitterness. It was bad enough I'd gotten a college degree and she hadn't. Now I'd married a non-Italian, moved 350 miles away, was raising her grandchildren without her influence, and wasn't giving her enough attention. The stress affected me. Insomnia began. It would become a problem off and on for years. Restless nights caused Gary to lose sleep too as he'd nudge my shoulder to try to settle me down. I'd wake up in the middle of the night with a jolt, sitting up in bed–my heart racing, breathless with a dry throat. I'd be drenched in sweat–even before menopause–and have to wash up in the bathroom and change my nightgown.

I'd have dreams about my mother criticizing me. I was talking back to Mom but the words weren't coming out of my mouth. I'd miss the bus. I lost my syllabus. I couldn't find my classroom. The semester was ending and I hadn't completed my assignments. My teeth fell out. I was driving the car naked. I was trying to cross an icy intersection. I didn't need a therapist to explain I had feelings of inadequacy. I thought I'd never measure up.

"You know, every time you hang up the phone with your mother, you're crying," Gary had said after one particular call.

"Am I?" Once he brought it to my attention, I realized how depleted I'd felt after those calls.

"Yes. I don't know what to tell you," he said, hugging me.

"She exhausts me. I can't take all her negative energy."

Mom had all day to ponder what I should and shouldn't do as a parent. I had barely enough time for a haircut. She'd been a traditional stay-at-home mom focused on housekeeping and taking care of her family and I was making my way as a career woman while juggling two children in day care. I felt a constant push-pull in my thirties. When I was at the office, I wanted to be home with my children. When I was home with my children, I wanted to go to work. Guilt grabbed hold of me in both places. I loved working but wished for more flexibility and vacation time.

Meanwhile, Mom and Dad had bought a beach cottage and started spending more time at the shore where they would eventually retire. In my mind, they had a new lease on life to indulge themselves in their new beachside community. Mom found a whole new world there and made lots of friends, yet the worry about Jimmy was never far from the surface.

Finally, one day Mom called me at work (something I asked her not to do unless it was an emergency). It was the day after she and Dad had returned home from a winter visit. We had driven into Boston together with their first grandchild. I imagined her sitting in her spot at the kitchen table with her feet up on a chair smoking a cigarette and sipping coffee.

"I want to tell you one thing," she said. This was her pattern: She'd think and evaluate and judge before calling with criticism. One thing was never just one thing.

"What, Mom?" I was standing in my office feeling anxious about a meeting I had to attend.

"When you take Kristin out, you need to put a hat on her at all times." I could hear her exhale a puff of smoke. "Make sure her ears are covered."

"That's why you called me at the office?" I said gritting my teeth and trying not to explode.

"Well, yes. It's been bothering me."

"Mom," I said as calmly as I could, "your job is to enjoy your grandchild. That's all you have to do. You don't have to keep giving me lectures. Just be a grandmother and try to have fun." I attempted to cut the conversation short, tired of being criticized my entire life with her "You should have . . ." comments. But Mom persisted.

"I can't help it, Joyce. When I see something wrong, I have to tell you. You know, you should be grateful I'm here to tell you things. My mother never gave me any advice. I only wished she'd have spoken up."

I hung up and walked outside for a burst of cold winter air. On the way home that night, I kept replaying the phone call with Mom in my head. Always, the shoulda, woulda, coulda messages from Mom. Was there nothing I could do right? Both hands gripped the wheel as I seethed on the poorly lit, two-lane road. Before I knew it, the car veered right onto a gravel patch. It jolted me from my distraught state as I narrowly avoided plummeting into a ditch.

Just when I thought we'd had a lovely family visit, she'd throw a wet blanket on me. My sisters and I had a greeting card we sent and re-sent to each other when we were young mothers. It depicted a caricature of a large woman hunched over wearing an overcoat and a small hat. The message inside read: *She came. She criticized. She left.* Lynne and Alison had their own ways of dealing with Mom. Alison could snap back with a retort, like "Get over it, Mom." Lynne would let Mom talk and then hang up and then call me with a "Guess what Mom said . . ." voice of exasperation. My sisters and I agreed that the unflattering parts of Mom's personality were becoming exaggerated with the stress of Jimmy getting older and the three of us too busy with our own families and jobs to help out.

Even though Mom was only fifty-nine when her first grandchild arrived, she felt late to the role because her friends and relatives had already experienced the joy of grandparenthood.

"You know," she said to me one day, "this should have happened to me ten years ago."

"Really, Mom?" I answered defiantly while cradling my baby. "Would you have preferred I got knocked up by a Drexel Hill hood back then so you could be a grandparent earlier?"

Nevertheless, she played the role her way. When the family

got together, she laughed when being entertained by her first grandchild. Mom hugged and cuddled with her grandchildren only in small doses. She wasn't at ease with them as babies the way my father was. Dad proudly pushed the stroller. Mom walked beside it. She might push the baby in the swing three times before moving aside for me to continue so she could light up a cigarette. Mom was always in observation and judgment mode. If I told her my baby tasted a banana for the first time, she'd quickly ask, "You didn't give her the whole banana, did you?" It got to the point where I called my mother-in-law to say, "Guess what Kristin did today?" I'd report about her singing the alphabet song or playing with a new toy and my mother-in-law would giggle and say, "Isn't that wonderful?" I regretted Mom missing out on the gift of my daily stories but I couldn't take the judgment.

Mom enjoyed her granddaughters more when they could talk to her. She loved teaching them new words. Mom helped them play dress-up when she visited at Christmas. She showed them how to make fresh lemonade at the beach; as toddlers, they'd stand on the kitchen chair next to her at the sink. She bought them thoughtful gifts and learning toys and wrote beautiful letters to them. One letter asked them to never smoke. She explained she'd done it to appear older and then became addicted. Her lesson worked.

My mother's definition of parenting differed from mine. She focused more on responsibility and sacrifice and less on the joy of parenting. At age thirty-three, I aimed for more joy as a parent. I went down the sliding board with my kids, held their hands while ice-skating and would lay on the floor to do puzzles. They had to make their beds and keep their rooms clean but I didn't load them down with housework like vacuuming and dusting.

On the night I got home after the near-accident, I told Gary about the conversation with Mom and suddenly realized I'd been in a parent mode my whole life. At that moment the memory of Ms. Sisk flashed back.

Ms. Sisk, my high school psychology teacher, had long, straight brown hair parted in the middle and didn't wear make-up. She wore Earth Shoes and oversized sweaters on her thin frame. She assigned us to write a term paper after completing her lesson on transactional analysis and the three ego states. Students had to choose which ego state–parent, adult or child–to inhabit for the rest of their lives, if forced to, and explain why they chose the role.

I had trouble choosing between the parent and the adult role because they seemed similar to me. It never occurred to me to choose the child role. I couldn't relate to the pleasure, recreation, or spontaneity associated with that ego state. That joie de vivre was for other families, not mine. Sure, my family had enjoyed the pool club, down the shore in Ocean City, Sunday drives to the Philadelphia airport, spending holidays with my cousins, playing basketball in our driveway. Yet a veil of seriousness enveloped our family along with a strict code of responsibility. My parents were raised during the Depression and the struggle to make ends meet and live frugally never left their psyche. More impactful was their constant worry about Jimmy.

Ms. Sisk defined the adult role as the pursuit of objective reality. After some deliberation, I chose to write about the adult role because it matched my personality and how I naturally behaved. Writing it came easily. When Ms. Sisk returned the graded paper with an "A" on the top right corner of the first page and no comments in the margins, I felt a sense of accomplishment. While descending the staircase after class, I flipped to the last page of the term paper and stopped midway down. There I read Ms. Sisk's singular note written in the form of a question: "What about just having fun?"

I was perplexed by her question but chose not to ask Ms. Sisk about it for fear of losing my grade. The next day, week, month passed as I wondered what her question meant. Years passed. I remained confused by her question. Not until I became a mother myself fifteen years later did I realize I had been acting in the adult ego state for as long as I could remember–probably since the first patterning session at age five.

I was in my early thirties the first time I said no to my mother. (Lynne rebelled in her twenties and Alison in her teens. Call me the late bloomer.) My mother could not relate to me as a career woman, placing my baby in the care of others. I desperately wanted Mom to fuss over my adorable daughter and simply embrace her long-awaited role as grandmother. I learned to selectively report news about my children to Mom because the criticism stung.

The distance helped me hide the resentment I'd begun to harbor toward Mom. I resented her for giving me all that responsibility for Jimmy in my childhood and the resentment grew. Shortly after I became a mother, we were on the porch of the beach cottage while her first grandchild napped.

"Why can't you stay longer?" she asked from the Adirondack chair. "I had so much fun today watching baby Kristin play in the sand."

"Mom, I only get so many vacation days at work and I have to plan those days off around my child care."

"I want to spend more time with my granddaughter. And

you live so far away."

"I know Mom. We'll visit when we can. I'm sorry we could only stay a few days but I have to get back to my job. Even now, I'm thinking about all the stuff I have to do when I get home."

She exhaled a cloud of smoke, relaxed her shoulders, then turned and locked eyes with me.

"You had too much responsibility when you were a child, Joyce."

When I reflect back to that moment, I believe her comment and facial expression conveyed equal parts regret and rationale. Finally, I'd heard my mother admit to what I'd felt for so many years but couldn't express. I felt sadness for the early loss of my youth.

How was I supposed to respond? A debate wouldn't have helped either of us. I realized she simply had to get it off her chest.

"I better go check on the baby," I said rising from my chair.

After the vacation, I returned to work, thankful for the familiarity and routine. A typical day began at 5:30. I'd dress and feed the girls, make the beds, prepare lunches, pack items for day care, bundle up, get my briefcase, drive through traffic for an 8:30 meeting, work nonstop at the office often without lunch, pick up the girls and chat with their caregivers, cook dinner, bathe the girls, read them a bedtime story, pay bills, do laundry, collapse. And this was with a loving and involved husband who shared parenting responsibilities, willingly stayed home with a sick baby, and took them to doctor's appointments. Sometimes I'd fall asleep while reading my children a bedtime story and they'd nudge me to continue. On the weekends, I'd get into a sour mood because it felt like I was taking away play time with my children to clean the house and prepare meals for the following week.

"Joyce, take it easy," Gary would say. "What are you doing? The house is clean already."

"I hate cleaning but I love a clean house."

"Then hire a cleaning lady," he suggested. I finally did and that helped.

By the time my daughters were preschoolers, resentment toward my mother reached another level. I thought about all those years taking care of Jimmy and doing housework and grieved for my lost childhood. Now, as an adult, I couldn't find time for joy, nor could I feel it. I feared telegraphing this to my daughters. When my husband planned a family vacation, I couldn't fully relax because I constantly worried my daughters might get sick or injured somehow, even though we were always together.

"When we get home . . ." I said more than once while on the beach at Cape Cod one summer, thinking of my never-ending to-do list.

"Joyce, ever since we got here, you've been telling me what you have to do when we get home," said Gary. "Can we relax and enjoy ourselves while we're here?"

I couldn't help myself. I'd been programmed my whole life to work, not play. I felt guilty indulging in free time knowing my parents weren't, knowing Jimmy was lonely and not being offered the same opportunities. Even though by now they had a beach cottage where they could unwind, I still felt guilty for not taking them on a vacation to Italy, not doing more for them, not being there to lighten their load.

My agitation grew. I'd finally found my husband who introduced me to recreational activities like skiing, skating, and golf, yet I felt undeserving of fun. It didn't help when one day

Mom was reflecting over a morning cup of coffee with me. She talked about a time when she saw a therapist off and on during her mid-forties. We were in the kitchen at the beach house and I was clearing the table.

"You know what Betty Lou said when I told her about you, Joyce?" she asked, tapping the cigarette ash into the ashtray.

I wasn't sure I wanted to hear and didn't answer. Instead, I stared at her and braced myself.

"She said you were the third parent."

I don't know how long Mom thought about it or why she decided to tell me but she was matter-of-fact about it.

I turned toward the sink, confounded. Heat rose within me. I couldn't look at her.

"She's right. You were the third parent." I could hear her exhale a puff of smoke. "I gave you too much responsibility. But it's okay. You're fine. And besides, you'll be stronger for it in the long run."

I could feel my cheeks flushing as I quickly stacked the remaining plates in the dishwasher.

"You're right, Mom. I'm fine," I answered flatly. She must have felt better but I went outside for fresh air and took a long walk. Gazing out at the bay, I wondered what my mother might have done differently with me had Jimmy not been so needy. How might my personality have been shaped? Would having fun ever come naturally to me?

27

Each year in Jimmy's early adulthood presented new challenges and difficulties for Mom and Dad: the onset of type II diabetes, sexual curiosity, school and employer meetings, the loss of his neighborhood friends who married or moved away.

"You don't know ..." she'd say gravely. "You don't know what goes on with Jimmy. Daddy and I don't tell you everything."

"Mom, you've told me plenty but I shouldn't have to know everything. What you and Daddy keep secret in your marriage is your business." At work I'd been taught to constructively confront problems, but I found myself avoiding conflict with my mother. I didn't want to hear about her post-menopausal problems. I didn't want to hear about the arguments she and Dad had about Jimmy or retirement or their finances. And I certainly didn't want to hear every single new challenge Jimmy presented for them. If I had let her, she'd have carped every day about something or other. I considered them lucky to own a beach house they could finally escape to.

In 1996, when she was sixty-four, Mom convinced Dad it was time to move away from Drexel Hill to Long Beach Island where they could retire. My sisters and I couldn't understand it but Mom was a visionary. They moved for Jimmy because the laws in New Jersey were favorable for people like him. It proved to be the right move because they made lots of wonderful friends and involved themselves in their new community. Mom became a member of the Garden Club and tinkered in her own garden with showy hollyhocks and plenty of perennials. Dad joined the Kiwanis Club and made friends there, hosting flea markets and fundraisers to benefit local children. They dined out a lot. The change of scenery both energized and relaxed them. Mom prayed she'd be blessed to live five years on the island. She got eleven.

After relocating to the island, she started thinking about where Jimmy would live after she and Dad died. Jimmy had turned forty and was working part-time at the Acme Supermarket collecting shopping carts and sweeping the front entrance. One afternoon she found Jimmy sitting alone on a bench facing the bay, a block from their home. She sat next to him and patted his hand the way she always did. They remained silent for a few moments before he turned to her.

"What's going to happen to me?" he asked.

His comment pierced her heart. He was wondering where he'd go, live, whom he'd be with. People assume that individuals with intellectual limitations have emotional limitations as well. Not true. It's harder to determine what those emotions are, and some people, like Jimmy, who is a deep thinker, aren't expressive about how they feel inside. I'd witness this later in the years after Mom died when I tried to offer him comfort during his grief.

Jimmy saw my parents slowing down physically. Mom had stopped driving. Jimmy knew my sisters and I were busy managing careers and young families because we didn't call or visit him as frequently. His friends had gotten jobs, married, and moved on. His part-time job at the grocery store was unfulfilling. His social life consisted of joining my parents on day trips or an occasional dinner out with their friends. Like many of us, he was anticipating his future but didn't have a vision beyond the beautiful horizon on the bay.

On one of our many three-way telephone conversations, Lynne, Alison, and I talked about Jimmy's future and our fears.

"He could live here," said Lynne. "I have an extra bedroom and my town is a safe, family-oriented community."

"Or here," said Alison. "I have room, too."

Silence. I could feel myself shaking inside.

"Well, I have to tell you . . . I can't do it. I'm sorry but I just can't do it. I've done enough," I said, trying to hold back tears. I had flashbacks to the patterning table, to exercises in the basement, and to school hallways. My adolescence was difficult enough. I couldn't let Jimmy consume my adult life. Moreover, I wasn't going to impact my daughters' formative years by having their needy adult uncle live with us.

Lynne and Alison said they understood and although I couldn't see the expressions on their faces, I sensed they earnestly accepted my position on the issue. None of that mattered because Mom quickly shot down my sisters' notions.

"It will ruin your marriage," she said more than once to each of us. One time, when Lynne was ending a visit at my parents' house, she raised the topic again. "No!" said my mother emphatically.

However, Mom surmised at least one of Jimmy's sisters would live within driving distance of him. She figured one of us would take him to doctor appointments, sporting events, bowling, shopping, out to eat, and include him in our family dinners and holidays. Alison and Lynne had done a lot of driving for Jimmy when they still lived in the area before they married and started their own families. Mom and Dad were overwhelmed because caring for Jimmy as an adult became a full-time job again. My parents rarely spent time as a couple. Mom's expectation of continued assistance fell short when all three daughters moved away. This made her job of planning for his future more difficult.

Mom responded the way she usually did when faced with a difficult situation. First she cried. Then she smoked a lot of cigarettes, lost sleep, and got sick with a cold or flu. She'd recline on the couch for a week before springing back into action.

Mom hired a trusted attorney who gave my parents sound advice and helped them through that difficult transitional period of their lives. The attorney also pushed them to apply for all the benefits to which Jimmy was entitled. Mom and Dad had never bothered applying for disability benefits for Jimmy when he first became eligible. They thought it was for indigent people and they didn't want to be categorized as dependent on the state.

Until then, they had mainstreamed Jimmy as much as possible. They judged he was better off working a part-time job as a taxpaying citizen contributing to society. But by the time he turned forty, they realized they should have been obtaining those benefits all along. They could have had more support from the government and maybe even had time for themselves as a couple to travel. Now they had to apply to the state and explain why Jimmy should receive the benefits after not claiming them for the twenty-plus years he'd been eligible.

Mom was worried about the important meeting in front of a judge, a stranger who would determine their fate. I advised her to bring lots of documentation. She had always kept everything organized and retained every document over the years. She had files dating back to Jimmy's school days in the Upper Darby School District. On the day of the meeting, she brought in stacks of folders and a large shoebox containing important papers clipped and stapled, receipts, everything date stamped. At one point, the judge asked her for a particular document and she thumbed through the dense files to effortlessly retrieve it.

"Joyce, Daddy and I are so happy!" said Mom that night. "The judge awarded Jimmy disability benefits today."

"That's terrific, Mom!"

"What a relief," she sighed. "The judge said Jimmy can keep his part-time hours at the Acme Supermarket, too."

"You did it again, Mom."

"Joyce . . ." she said lowering her voice to a serious tone, "I want to thank you."

"What for?"

"If it weren't for you coaching me and preparing me for this meeting, I don't know what the outcome would have been. I brought all those papers into the conference room like you told me to do. And I answered the questions concisely without volunteering information. The judge complimented me on how well-prepared I was."

I appreciated her sincerity and humility. It heartened me to know I had helped Mom this way. She didn't often thank me. I felt satisfied knowing I could still make a difference in Jimmy's life even though we lived far apart.

About this time, Jimmy qualified for respite care. Mom and Dad took him to the homes of licensed social workers for several weekends over a two-year period. Of course, the respite was for my parents as much as it was for Jimmy. They certainly needed the breaks. Jimmy was confused and scared. He asked why he was at a stranger's house instead of home or at least with one of his sisters. This was part of his transition plan to living without my parents.

Mom and Dad sat Jimmy down and explained their long-range plan for him.

"Ro, I don't know if he understands the terminology you're using."

"He understands. I'll talk to my son the way I'd talk to the pope," Mom said, insistent and proud.

They had to force a separation before they died. They were preparing Jimmy for a different routine and dependency on people other than family, namely social workers with an organization called The Arc.

The Arc is a national organization for people with intellectual and developmental disabilities. It was founded in 1950 by a small group of parents in the Midwest who wanted to build support and a community for their children. Back then, they'd heard the same advice from their doctors as my parents had: to institutionalize their children, which many people did at the time. However, these parents rallied around a common goal to have their children lead fulfilling lives in their own neighborhoods. Originally named the Association for Retarded Children (ARC), the organization changed its name to the Association for Retarded Citizens in 1973. Finally, in 1992, it was renamed The Arc. In the past sixty years, The Arc has worked with state and federal governments to pass legislation on behalf of special citizens like Jimmy. The only "R" word for them is respect.

Mom found a supervised apartment for Jimmy about forty-five minutes from their home, managed by a local chapter of

The Arc. It was a safe environment in a nice location. Jimmy was the first special needs adult to move in. The social workers helped my brother acclimate to his new environment. We all told Jimmy what a positive milestone this was for him but he had his doubts. He continued to ask why he couldn't live with one of his sisters.

"I have room in my house for Jimmy," offered Lynne to Mom.

"No, Lynne. I told you before. Promise me you will never take Jimmy away from his apartment," she said. "I worked too hard to make this happen. It's the best arrangement for him, and for you and your sisters. Trust me."

Jimmy kept saying he wanted to "come home." It tore us apart to hear this. In the first several months of his semi-independent living, he would go home to my parents' house on weekends. Over time, those visits became less frequent.

My parents were finally free of the daily struggle of parenting Jimmy but never free of the emotional burden. They still couldn't relax and they certainly weren't about to start traveling. They felt sad with and without him. That's when Mom's health started to decline. She fell into a deep depression and never really recovered.

The same week my parents moved Jimmy to his own apartment, I had a career milestone and was promoted to vice president. I'd worked hard to achieve the level of job responsibility but my pride was muted by the news of Jimmy's monumental move. Mom detailed the steps of relocating him and conveyed her worry.

"I hope he makes new friends there," she said on the phone.

"Sure he will, Mom."

"I hope he adjusts. You know, he's used to my cooking.

And he likes his own space," she continued between drags of a cigarette.

"Mom, this is the right thing. You're brave to do this. Jimmy will be fine. It will take time, but he'll be fine. You and Daddy have done a remarkable job."

"I hope people will be kind to him," she said, her voice trailing off.

She talked a lot that first week and I listened. It took another week before I told her my news, almost apologetically. How could I celebrate my success with my parents, knowing their anguish and Jimmy's fear and confusion?

"Vice president," she said quietly. "Well. That's great news."

"Thanks, Mom."

"You know, Joyce. If Jimmy hadn't been born brain-damaged, he'd have been the smartest of all my children. And he'd have been the most successful."

She'd say this several more times and I never knew what to make of it. Each time I heard her words, they stung. As if I hadn't done enough, studied enough, worked hard enough to achieve my goals and make her proud. What happened to the mother who believed in my potential? I flashed back to a scene at age seventeen when she, Dad, and I had finished touring a college. Mom had asked Dad to pull into a new subdivision so she could tour a McMansion being constructed. As the three of us stood in the empty master bedroom overlooking an expansive manicured lawn, Dad wondered about the type of couple who could afford such a house.

"My dear," he'd said to me, "it's just as easy to marry a rich man as it is to marry a poor man." He chuckled but I knew he was serious.

"Oh, Babe," said Mom.

"Well, it's true," he continued. "I think one day Joyce is going to marry a vice president," he said proudly, indicating he'd consider it an accomplishment.

Mom stepped away from the window and said, "Someday Joyce is going to *be* a vice president." I don't know who was more startled by her proclamation, Dad or me.

After Mom died, Dad would restate Mom's earlier remark whenever Jimmy surprised him with a fact about current events. "Your mother always said Jimmy would have been the smartest of all of you . . ."

Eventually I learned to dismiss the comment, figuring it made Mom and Dad feel faultless to imagine Jimmy's potential as a fully, able-minded individual. It wouldn't be until I reached midlife when I realized they were still grieving the loss of a healthy son.

As my parents detached themselves from primary caregiving of Jimmy, I learned more about parenthood, mostly by reading and observing. I hesitated asking Mom for parenting advice because she took a negative, cautionary approach. The "should have" comments seemed aimed at what I did wrong or what she could do better than me. I felt judged by her all the time and then found myself being cautious and afraid to use my own trusted judgment. My daughters would be laughing down the slide at the playground or riding bikes and the first directions I'd give them were "Be careful" and "Watch out" before "Whee!" As they got older, I'd add "Have fun" to words of caution whenever they'd go out with friends. That's what I had wanted to hear from my mother.

At times I'd catch myself adopting Mom's traits. I didn't smile easily and grew scared because I didn't want to live my life sad. Mom had a way of sucking the life right out of the room with her negative energy that I believe was rooted in sadness and lost opportunity. She'd felt slighted, as if she'd been dealt a bad hand. Growing up she felt overshadowed by her older brother and sister. She never got to go to college and she had a burden unlike her peers. She bemoaned how her friends' mothers had helped them and hers didn't. She frequently mentioned how her own mother, while considerate to all her grandchildren, never reached out to support Jimmy, the only grandson and the namesake of my grandfather. Resentment stayed with Mom and it turned to depression, extreme caution, and a roster of ailments: headaches lasting for days, neuralgia, gastro-intestinal disorders, gallstones, arthritis, anemia, a high sedimentation rate indicating inflammation and/or infection in the body, and heart disease which finally caught up with her at age seventy-six.

I couldn't let resentment and sadness overshadow all the goodness in my life. I couldn't tolerate her glass-half-empty personality dragging me down. I'd been attracted to my husband for the fun he brought through travel and his "Let's go!" attitude. I wanted him and my children to embrace joy and to be spontaneous. And I wanted to do the same even though it didn't come naturally to me.

A turning point came after my second child was born. Mom had barely acknowledged her birth. She didn't call regularly and instead stayed at the beach house for six weeks before meeting her new granddaughter. In that time I experienced postpartum depression. Gary finally told me he couldn't be objective and urged me to seek help. A few sessions of talk therapy helped.

I tried to remain aware of when my mood dipped or negativity set in. I also promised to keep myself as healthy as possible, particularly after experiencing anemia and skin rashes as a teenager. Yoga and my coveted morning walks always cleared the cobwebs. They have been key to my mental well-being. I've loaded up on fruits, vegetables, and yogurt and cut out meat in an effort to lead a healthy lifestyle.

Yet, as different as I claim to be from my mother, I share many of her behaviors. Like her, I prefer solitary activities like reading, gardening, and crossword puzzles. I value writing and like to use pretty stationery to pen letters in cursive. I consult books for answers and often say, "I read it somewhere." I correct my daughters' grammar ("My friends and I are going . . ."). I am specific and particular when giving instructions in the kitchen (separate cutting boards for vegetables, chicken, and bread) and with housekeeping (match the corners of the afghan neatly before folding it over the couch). I am constantly cleaning out closets and drawers. I don't like crowds and loud places. Although I did enjoy DisneyWorld, I only tolerated other amusement parks for the sake of my young daughters. When *Jeopardy!* is on TV, I don't answer the phone or participate in any conversation. I pull the skin back on the sides of my face with my thumb and forefinger and say, "If I could have a facelift." I hold a sandwich the way Mom did: elbows on the table, knuckles in the palm of the hand holding the bread between bites. Like she did, I even eat the sandwich over the cutting board without transferring it to a plate when I'm too hungry.

Moreover, I set a beautiful holiday table and display fresh flowers and plants around a meticulously clean house. "Put a plant in every room. They emit oxygen, absorb toxins, and keep the air fresh," she'd say. I'm super-organized, always planning, and my meatballs are almost as tasty as hers.

28

After thirty years in the human resources profession, I co-managed the acquisition of my last employer by a Fortune 500 company and then voluntarily stepped away. At the time, I hadn't known I was essentially retiring from corporate life. I lounged on the porch all summer reading voraciously.

Two months earlier I'd been diagnosed with psoriatic arthritis. Redness and swelling began in the fourth toe of my left foot and spread to the big toe. The podiatrist called it "sausage toe" and prescribed anti-inflammatory medication. My feet reminded me of Fred Flintstone's and I had to wear a clunky black boot with Velcro straps until the swelling subsided. Walking without throbbing pain was impossible especially when the arthritis spread to my other foot. My favorite high-heels and wedges remained untouched at the bottom of the closet.

My sister Alison told me I'd literally run myself into the ground and I began to think she was right. I couldn't sleep. I lost my appetite and became depressed. My doctor told me if I didn't want to take antidepressants then I'd have to release natural endorphins by developing a disciplined exercise routine.

I'd never been an athlete and exercising or swimming at

the Y didn't interest me. One day I sauntered out of a favorite café finally fitting into a pair of sandals when I noticed a new yoga studio in town. *This is my speed,* I thought. I started off with beginner classes and found my quad muscles quickly. My triceps burned. My hip joints ached. My wrists hurt. I couldn't balance on one foot for more than a few breaths. I wondered if I'd ever find the downward dog position restful. I had to learn how to calm myself with yoga breathing—matching the length of each inhalation with the length of each exhalation.

Despite initial soreness and self-consciousness, I continued going to the studio. I started to feel better, nimble, and lighter on my feet. I climbed stairs instead of taking the elevator, stood up straighter, lost a few pounds without trying, and experienced a sense of inner calm. I drove slower and wasn't agitated by waiting in line or in traffic. My body grew stronger and healthier. I slept better and haven't had a flare-up of arthritis since I began practicing yoga.

Three job offers came quickly but none of them excited me. I didn't want to commit myself to a new employer then find myself wanting to get out of an intolerable situation. Calls from former colleagues came and they'd ask, "Can I pick your brain?" After one too many of those calls for free advice, I decided to set up a small consulting practice. It suited me at the time and afforded me the flexibility I needed while still using my professional skills and generating an income.

In addition to being able to finally book a hair appointment in the middle of the week, I also had more time to make the 350-mile drive to spend time with my parents. I played nurse and housekeeper for a couple of weeks after Dad's bypass operation and Mom's stroke.

"I'm afraid of having another stroke," she said to me when I stayed for a week to help her recover.

"Mom, you're doing great. Keep moving. Remember what the doctor said? Circulate. Circulate."

While Mom was struggling to improve her health, little by little I assumed an administrative role regarding Jimmy's care. I developed relationships with his social workers, maintained documentation, fielded calls, and problem-solved.

There were a few crises to be managed. Jimmy was taken by ambulance from the grocery store more than once. He fell and gashed his forehead leaving him with a Harry Potter scar. He went into diabetic shock after drinking a liter of orange soda. When I learned Mom never went to the hospital to see Jimmy after one particular episode, I knew it was the beginning of the end for her.

"I think my mother has thrown in the towel," I said to a friend during our Sunday morning walk. I sensed Mom had resigned from life and didn't have any more fight left in her. I also sensed there was nothing I could do to help her or inspire her to put up a fight. Oddly, I felt lighter for it.

Mom was tired. She wouldn't come to the phone. I heard the fatigue in Dad's voice from his round-the-clock caregiving. I could picture him looking at Mom while on the phone with me while she waved her pointer finger and shook her head "No."

"She's sleeping now," he'd say. I'd let it go without pressing him for details. There are certain times when a child shouldn't intrude on the privacy of their parents' marriage and this was one of them. I knew Dad would just cover up with an "Everything's fine" answer if I quizzed him about Mom's health.

Mom isolated herself those last few months. The few times she did come to the phone she'd say "I'm tired" and then hand the phone back to Dad. Although she'd recovered from the stroke, she was tired of trying to get well, tired of fighting for Jimmy's rights, tired of being tired. Her breathing was labored and her sed rate (an inflammation marker) remained high. Her last months were slow, sedentary, antisocial, and full of fear.

Mom and Dad met with the heart surgeon who described how he'd repair the aneurysms and aorta. He explained the risks and added that one option would be to do nothing.

"Ro, you don't have to go through with the operation," said Dad.

"I'm afraid one of the aneurysms will burst and I'll die in agony," she'd said. That's how Mom's brother died—an aneurysm burst on his eighty-first birthday. Mom felt compelled to go through with it, claiming she couldn't go on like she had those last few months living an unproductive, unfulfilling life.

Mom's heart surgery was scheduled for a Friday morning. I sensed it would be fatal. I believe she thought she'd rather die on the operating table than risk having a protracted and painful death.

"I think I should pack black," I said to my husband the night before driving to New Jersey. "I have a bad feeling." The premonition felt like a dark cloud looming over me.

"Try to be positive," he answered. "Pack comfortable clothes if you'll be hanging around the hospital a lot."

The six-hour drive gave me plenty of time to think and worry. Even on that sunny, cool mid-November day, I sensed a dark cloud traveling with me over the car as my thoughts ran rampant. I was alone again, on a mission. If Mom made it through, she'd need rehab. Would she cooperate with physical and occupational therapy or would she be too weak and tired? She did well with rehab after her stroke earlier in the year but then she fell back into her sedentary lifestyle. She gained weight and slept a lot. She barely left the house and turned down social invitations. She rarely came to the phone when my sisters and I called. She did, however, meet with two lifelong friends at a restaurant for lunch saying she wanted to see them before her surgery.

"I don't know when I'll see them again, and I wanted to have a nice lunch together," she said to me afterward, on one of the few times she came to the phone those last months. It sounded like she planned to say her goodbyes that day.

The hours passed while I drove in solitude through Connecticut, New York, and New Jersey without music. Only the hum of my car, highway traffic, and the grinding of eighteen-wheelers kept me company. So many other trips on this route were driven with my family in eager anticipation of lazy days on Long Beach Island, outdoor showers, bike rides, and ice cream. Now those happy images were eclipsed by anxiety.

Could Dad continue taking care of Mom himself? He'd already been managing a heavy burden for the past several years since his own double bypass, tending to her every need: constant trips to the pharmacy for multiple prescriptions, cooking meals, doing laundry, chauffeuring to doctor's appointments and, toward the end, bathing and toileting her. Would there be more surgeries for Mom? How would my sisters and I handle all this? Since Lynne and Alison had full-time jobs and I had a flexible, part-time consulting practice, I figured a lot of the logistics and communications would fall to me. I made a mental note to investigate visiting nurse options and home care. I even started thinking about what I might write in a eulogy, knowing the task would fall to me.

I only stopped once, for gas and a bathroom break. I ate a peanut butter and jelly sandwich and nibbled on an apple while driving.

My sisters and father were optimistic about the surgery. I spoke like I believed there would be a positive outcome but privately remained the pessimistic realist. While waiting in the hospital room before pre-op, everyone was chatting. The medical staff gave Mom papers to sign and joked with her, presumably to lighten the mood. She smiled at all the attention. I stepped forward and assumed the business mode of interviewer.

"Will you please explain to me the procedures you'll be doing? How many times have you performed this type of surgery? How long do you expect her to be in surgery? What are the risks?"

"Joyce," my mother said from the narrow hospital bed, trying to quell me. "The doctors know what they're doing." She always held physicians in high regard, as practically infallible. You'd think she'd have had a dubious attitude after interactions with Jimmy's pediatricians and Dr. Spitz but she didn't. I, on the other hand, treated the doctors as professionals who were capable of making mistakes.

"I know, Mom. I want to understand exactly what they'll be doing."

My family chuckled at my pointedness but I remained serious. I didn't think it was appropriate for the medical staff to be making jokes. I felt offended and insulted. This was a serious matter and I recognized it might well have been my last moments with Mom. The doctors and nurses seemed like interlopers in what I considered a sacred family affair.

"Who's going to call my sister?" asked Mom.

"I will," answered Lynne.

"Who's going to call Claire?" she asked about her lifelong friend.

"I will," I answered.

"Who's going to call Dolores Kornblatt?" Mom persisted. She continued asking who'd call a few more special people in her life. We assured her we had everything under control.

Finally, from the other side of the curtain came the voice of her roommate asking, "Who's going to call Obama?"

That was my mother's last hearty laugh. We all laughed with her.

When she got up to use the bathroom, she put on her slippers and paused by the bedside where I stood guard. I tried to remain composed but kept wringing and folding my hands. Mom had the most tranquil expression on her face I'd ever seen. Her expression struck me because, off and on through the years, I remember her brows furrowed with worry and anger. This time she took my hands and looked me straight in the eye. Wordlessly, I sensed her communicate, "I've done all I can for you, Joyce." I'll never forget that moment or the visage of peace in my mother's eyes. I knew the end was near and I intuited she did, too.

The nurses stopped the gurney before the swinging doors leading into the operating room.

"Mrs. Poggi?" asked the nurse, pronouncing the name correctly in an accented voice.

"That's me."

"Is that an Italian name?"

"Yes it is," Mom answered proudly.

"Where I come from it means 'handsome'."

"Do you hear that, Babe?" she turned to Dad, smiling. "You've been handsome all these years."

She took Lynne's hand first and drew her near. Face to face, Mom said, "You're a good daughter. I love you. Stay close," pointing to Alison and me. She repeated the same exact words to me as obviously rehearsed, then to Alison, before we kissed her and told her we loved her, too. After we each had our moment with Mom, we gave her private time with Dad.

The surgery took longer than expected. Alison crocheted half an afghan in the waiting room. Lynne went back and forth to the cafeteria for snacks and drinks. Dad watched TV mindlessly, shifted in his seat, stood to stretch his legs, and paced.

"She should have been out by now," Dad said a few times, tapping the face of his watch.

As the communicator in the family, I received and made calls to the nurses during the nearly seven-hour ordeal. The tones of their voices signaled trouble, but I didn't communicate that to Dad. I had to conceal the truth and convey hope. The truth was Mom's heart had significantly more damage than they had expected, a result of sixty years of cigarettes.

She went into cardiac arrest as they were transferring her from the operating table to the gurney for post-op. They resuscitated her and moved her back onto the operating table to open her up again. I didn't tell Dad this until she was out of surgery.

We visited Mom as she lay motionless for the next two days. Finally, Lynne and Alison drove home through a snowstorm. Dad and I remained at the hospital all day Sunday until we too finally decided to go home. A few minutes before reaching Dad's house, we crossed over the causeway bridge and I had an extrasensory perception.

There's a point on the bridge where your car rises and all you can see is sky. The bay and marinas and summer cottages fall away beneath your line of vision. When we crested at the gloomy hour of dusk, I experienced something transcendental. My heart fluttered. I startled myself when I suddenly drew in a breath. In that moment, I sensed Mom rising from the earth to the celestial sky on my horizon.

Less than an hour after returning to Dad's house, I was putting spaghetti into boiling water when the phone rang. I didn't recognize the caller ID immediately and almost chose to ignore the call when I realized it could be the nurse.

"Joyce, you and your father should come to the hospital now."

The dark county roads were eerily empty on the forty-five minute drive. Dad sat in the passenger seat and periodically rested his left hand on my right hand. We both knew what we'd face when we got there but figured we should hold on to a sliver of hope.

"Maybe we'll get there in time," I said, trying to be optimistic.

"Maybe."

"If we don't, are you prepared, Daddy?"

"Yes. I know."

Another pause. We stared through the windshield into the still night. I drove cautiously on the empty county road with pine barrens on either side, alert for deer or other critters jumping out from the woods. But the only sound came from the dull hum of the car engine.

"Daddy, I'll stay as long as you want me to," I said.

"Thank you, honey. I need you. We'll have a lot to do this week."

When we entered the ICU, I noticed a petite hospital worker slipping a large plastic sleeve over the IV pole outside of Mom's room. We approached the doorway but the nursing supervisor stretched her arms out wide to redirect Dad and me into a small conference room and tell us what we already knew.

"Your wife died twenty minutes ago," the nurse said. "The doctor massaged her heart for almost an hour. It was her time."

I'd heard the empty phrase "it was her time" on TV and at people's wakes and always considered it a ridiculous platitude. Now here it was being served up to me.

While Dad spent a few moments with Mom's body, I stood in the doorway shaking, knowing he needed privacy. I saw him take her hand and heard him whisper before finally bending down to kiss her. He kept his face close to hers.

The petite hospital worker stopped her cleaning and stayed with me. She took my hands and held them. "I'm sorry," she said softly in an undistinguishable accent. I wish I could have thanked that gentle woman for her kindness. She made my numbness momentarily subside by giving me unexpected comfort.

Dad turned and let me have time with Mom. I kissed her forehead and was startled by its coolness. "Mom," I wept. "Mommy. Mommy. Mommy." I don't know how the childhood version of 'Mommy' surfaced from my lips but it did. I looked at her and saw peace. Her frown lines had disappeared. All the medical equipment had been removed from the room. No more wires. No more beeping. No more IVs. Only Mom's body lying in front of the windows, the curtains left open on the cool November night. How do I leave? How much time do we spend here? I turned to Dad and his chest was right there for me to bury my face. He wrapped his arms around me and led me out of the room.

My phone rang as Dad and I walked through the hospital lobby. It immediately sent me into crisis management mode. Something clicked in my head. *Time to act. Don't cry.* In my work life, I was known as a driver–an employee who is action-oriented to produce results versus an employee who relies on an expressive personality for success. But even long before then, Jimmy unknowingly taught me how to remain calm during a storm. When he chipped his tooth on the bottom of the pool, he remained unfazed. When he had his wisdom teeth pulled and, later, abdominal surgery, he only asked when and what he'd be able to eat. When our grandparents died, he asked a few questions about the body and then gave his typical "Oh" or "That's a shame." I don't remember him crying over anything. He'd do as my mother said and continue his day without a fuss. Except when the Flyers lost, he didn't complain when something didn't go the way he wanted. Who knows what emotions lay beneath the surface? At the time, I didn't consider if Jimmy felt deeply about matters or if it was simply the fact that he was a boy and boys didn't emote. As I'd observe in our adulthood, Jimmy is a deep thinker, just like Mom and me. He expresses himself in his own way and I'd often have to read between the lines.

"She's gone." I'd repeat the story multiple times when making all the calls later that evening to my aunts and Mom's closest friends.

Afterward I lay in bed staring at the ceiling, waiting for the tears. I felt numb. All I kept thinking was *my mother is dead, my mother is gone, my mother died.* In the small guest bedroom, I lay under the covers shifting my legs, feeling alone in the world. The earth kept spinning and life existed outside those four walls but my body felt leaden and at the same time detached from the mattress. Even though I'd predicted my mother's death, I had to keep repeating to myself, *my mother is dead,* to know it was true. And then, like my habitual self, I started a mental checklist of all the things I'd have to do in the coming days.

Dad moved through the next week in a haze. I made calls to the hospital and the funeral director. I drove Dad to the funeral home and helped him make all the decisions you're suddenly faced with when a family member dies. I made arrangements for cremation, ordered flowers, wrote the obituary, wrote the eulogy, and coordinated travel arrangements for the family. I made sure Dad ate and rested. I listened to and watched his friends come and go and hold Dad's hand and cry. With Mom's phone book on my lap, I repeated the same story to more acquaintances and neighbors. Things had to get done. I'd grieve later.

I went into my parents' bedroom to retrieve a shirt to iron for Dad. I stood there in the stillness and semi-darkness. The sun filtered through a gap in the green damask curtains. I went to Mom's dresser. It matched the rest of the bedroom set her parents gave as a wedding present. I tugged open the top drawer where she kept her jewelry and inhaled the smell of old mahogany. I fingered a pearl bracelet we'd given her for her sixtieth birthday–four strands, one for each child. My fingertips grazed the vintage earrings and pins she kept in a large velvet divider. After a couple of minutes, I pushed the drawer shut and startled myself when I caught the sad, colorless face in the mirror. I'd aged. Descending the stairs, my knees buckled halfway down.

"Things. Mom's things," I whispered. I wiped my eyes with the heels of my hands and sat there. Just things, the earrings and necklaces she wore. She touched them. Those things are now my treasures: her antique hairpin holder, pearl bracelet, beaded eyeglass chain, and make-up case. I touch the things she touched.

Dad stood in the middle of the living room, still in shock. I slowly treaded down the rest of the staircase, went to him and buried my head in his chest again. When he wrapped his arms around me, I felt his chest heave and heard a low whimper. We felt pain and comfort together in each other's arms.

"C'mon. Let's go," he said. We had to go back to the funeral home to verify her body before it was transferred to the crematory.

I kept a step behind Dad as we walked in.

"Dad," I said approaching the front door. "This is one thing I can't do with you. I'm sorry."

He shook his head and let out a half laugh the way he did whenever addressing an uncomfortable situation. I found it incongruous yet, at the same time, it relaxed me.

"That's okay, honey. I can do it by myself." He left with the funeral director while I sat erect on the edge of a red velvet chair in a heavily draped parlor. Five minutes later, Dad crossed the hallway, shaking his head.

"It's a good thing you didn't come with me," said Dad with a titter. Jutting out his thumb, he continued, "I told the funeral director here that's not Rosemarie. It may have been her body, but this is Rosemarie," he said holding out a picture he'd kept in his wallet for years. The photo showed Mom at age twenty-nine when she modeled in a local fashion show. "This was my wife. Wasn't she beautiful?" he asked admiring the old photo.

On the way back, we stopped at Target to buy an outfit for me to wear to the funeral.

"Is this okay?" I asked Dad, coming out of the dressing room in a pleated black skirt and tweed jacket.

"You look nice," he said with a rueful smile.

After several restless nights and two long days of making

funeral arrangements, I tried to relax in the living room with Dad over a cup of tea. I tucked my feet under me on the couch, covered myself with an afghan, and let Dad talk. I still didn't allow myself to falter. I decided I could do that on my own later in the privacy of my home. Dad needed me to be strong. It didn't seem right he should comfort me when I had a family to return home to who would comfort me.

"I'd have taken care of her here," he said, tapping the arm of his easy chair.

"I know, Dad."

"I really thought she'd pull through it."

"She was strong in a lot of ways."

"When I saw the dialysis machine," he said with widened eyes. "She wouldn't have wanted to go through dialysis."

"That would have been awful."

"You know," he mused, "this past summer we took a drive up to the lighthouse, your mother and I. Her favorite ride. She loved it up there. She used to say, 'Pull in here, Babe' to me. Up and down every street so she could admire the pretty houses and gardens. She knew the names of all the flowers." He paused and stared out the window. "Anyway, a few months ago, we were driving home and she said to me, ,'I'm dying, you know.' I said, 'Oh, Rosemarie, stop it.' 'Yes, Babe, I'm dying. This is the end for me. I know it.'" Then he looked at me. "That's what your mother said."

As he told me this story, I witnessed clarity in his expression. He moved from thinking it was just my mother being overdramatic to a slow realization that she had been right.

~

One of the hardest things I had to do was tell Jimmy.

Dad and I drove to the supermarket where Jimmy worked to get him before the end of his shift.

"Get in, Jimmy. We'll drive you home," Dad said.

"How's Mom?" he asked, climbing into the back seat. He had known her surgery was several days earlier but we'd only told him over the phone that she was still recovering in the hospital.

"Mom's in the hospital," Dad said. Nothing else was said during the five-minute drive.

When we got to Jimmy's apartment, we went into his bedroom to avoid the possibility of being interrupted in the sparse living room he shared with two other residents. I turned on a lamp. Dad spoke first.

"Sit down, Jimmy."

I sat down next to my brother on the edge of the bed while Dad stood facing him. I prepared myself for Jimmy to break down and didn't know if I'd cry with him.

"Mommy didn't make it through the surgery. She died, Jimmy."

"You're kidding." *Oh my God, this isn't what somebody says when they hear their mother dies.* But it was exactly what he said—clearly a gut reaction—so I contained my shock.

"Mommy's gone," said Dad.

"Oh." Jimmy stared at Dad for a moment with his mouth wide open and hands on either side of him resting on the navy blue comforter.

Barely a minute passed. I didn't know whom to console. My brother was in a state of shock and my father didn't know what to do or how to comfort Jimmy, so he distracted himself.

"Now, where's your suit jacket?" Dad asked, turning to open

the closet door. "Do you have a clean white shirt, Jimmy? You need a white shirt for the funeral," he said, pushing hangers aside.

I thought my father should have been hugging Jimmy or crying or saying something other than talking about what he should wear to the funeral. I quickly realized this was too hard for my father. Mom had always been the communicator. I had to step in.

"Dad," I said, getting up from the bed and guiding him toward the door. "Why don't you go downstairs and tell The Arc staff? I'll stay here with Jimmy and get his suitcase ready. Wait for us in the lobby." I saw Dad's shoulders relax under the coat he hadn't bothered to remove.

"Okay," he said, sounding relieved. "I'll go downstairs."

I sat back down on the bed, shifted toward Jimmy, and took his hands in mine.

"Jimmy, are you okay?"

"Yeah."

He appeared numb. He sat still on the bed and stared at the opposite wall. I felt compelled to talk but didn't know what to say.

"Mom's heart was diseased, Jimmy. The doctors couldn't make it better."

Stillness.

"Mom loved you very much. She was so proud of you." I stayed next to him and put both my arms around his shoulders. He let me hug him but he didn't hug back. He didn't cry and neither did I. We sat there, alone together in silence.

At the end of my mother's service, I was collecting sympathy cards. As people shuffled out, I turned and saw Jimmy kneeling in front of the polished cedar box with Mom's cremains. I immediately thought I should go kneel with him until I heard him mumble something. I held back, realizing he needed a moment by himself. I watched and waited patiently, fighting the urge to join him. Then I saw him gently tap the lid and whisper in his distinctively husky voice, "Bye-bye." I'd never heard his voice filled with sadness like that. I'd never witnessed such a tender expression from Jimmy. He rose and turned toward me with a questioning look on his face. My heart broke for him. I walked to him and hugged him. We were alone together again.

In the following months, Jimmy had a noticeable lack of expression over Mom's death. He never cried in front of us and his social workers said they didn't see any obvious signs of grief.

"Jimmy, do you miss Mom?" I'd ask on the phone.

"Not really."

"No? Do you think about her?"

"Sometimes."

"What do you think about, Jimmy?"

"I don't know . . ."

I couldn't get anything out of him. I didn't know if he didn't miss her because he hadn't seen much of her the last year or if he felt empty. She'd been depressed since the stroke eight months prior and isolated herself from family and friends. When Mom opted not to see Jimmy in the hospital after he'd fallen and gashed his head, a red flag signaled to me she'd checked out emotionally. It was easy to refrain from friends but to refrain from Jimmy told me she was letting go of life. I don't know what her purposeful distance signaled to Jimmy.

Jimmy could have been feeling guilty because, according to Dad, he acted rudely to Mom during their last visit together a couple of weeks before she died. Mom and Dad had driven to visit Jimmy and take him out to lunch. Mom admonished him for burping out loud and Jimmy got indignant.

"Jimmy, give me a hug before I leave," she said pulling him toward her. He leaned in and gave her a perfunctory tap on the back. Then he walked into his apartment without looking back. She cried all the way home.

All those tears. Tears of frustration, sadness, anger, bitterness, fear, hurt. All the love. All those years. She knew it might well be the last time she saw her son.

When I prepared to leave Dad's house after Mom's funeral, he hugged and thanked me.

"I don't know what I would have done without you, honey. You're just like your mother," he said.

My body tensed. I resisted the urge to say *I'm nothing like her!* I neither considered myself to be like Mom nor did I aspire to be like her. When I left Dad's embrace, a lump formed in my throat and tears filled my eyes. I opened the door to leave and a gust of cold November air whipped across my face.

On the six-hour drive back home, I had time to contemplate. What similarities did Dad see that I couldn't? We lived in separate generations. I'd graduated college and built a business career. I moved into my own apartment, bought my own couch, traveled, and waited until my thirties to marry and have children. Mom left her parents' house at age twenty to marry, never having lived on her own. She stayed home to raise a family while I juggled working full-time with two children in day care. She decorated her house with vintage crockery and shades of brown. Blues and greens adorn my rooms. Finally, I realized what Dad meant: In a crisis, I spring into action and get things done, just like Mom.

29

I don't remember my mother mourning the death of her mother. She may have cried privately but I never saw a display of grief, even at the funeral. Rather, after her mother died, I watched Mom scrub the kitchen tile in the row home where she grew up. As my first experience with death, I thought she should have been sitting on the couch holding her father's hand and crying. Instead, she had to channel her abundant nervous energy by doing something physical—cleaning.

In the months after Mom's death, I thought of her in quiet moments, often in the solitary act of housecleaning. The emptiness of dusting items she bought made me contemplative. That's when I'd weep, thinking of Mom, her illness and pain, the blurry gray of her passing. I didn't experience a gushing, painful grief. Because of that, I felt sad and guilty. I had mentally prepared myself for her passing the month before and specifically on that long drive to the hospital before her final surgery. The truth is that my mother hadn't been a part of my daily life. She hadn't been my confidante. I chose to keep a respectful distance between us because I couldn't cope with more criticism about my parenting skills, career, or home life. I'd had enough. I had decided to avoid any kind of conflict or opportunity for her to give me direction in order to keep peace. I kept our conversations general despite the fact that we both had deep thoughts about our own, sometimes strained, relationship. We both knew but never acknowledged the reason was due to Jimmy's impact on my past, present, and future.

More than seven years after Mom died, Dad and I sat in a café eating breakfast and chatting about a friend's son whom Dad felt was ignored by his parents.

"Just like we never paid any attention to you," Dad said.

I placed the fork on my plate, looked at him and waited.

"Your brother was so needy. Mommy had to spend all her time with him. But you knew. Somehow you knew. You understood and you adapted."

I sensed Dad needed absolution. All those years later, the facts may have bothered him more than they had bothered me.

"I'm okay, Dad. I did okay."

"You did more than okay. You did great."

His words made me feel lighter. No matter how old we get, a parent's recognition still matters.

I'd forgiven Mom for giving me too much responsibility and for the stinging comments she made. Eventually, the images of her anger and last sickly years gave way to my memory of her life as a deep, thoughtful, and vibrant woman. I recollected poignant scenes, such as the way I looked at her in surprise while unwrapping yet another thoughtful gift on Christmas or on my birthday. She exuded joy in giving, clasping her hands together and smiling with her chin tilted downward.

After the funeral I called Dad every day, sometimes two or three times, to check on him and try to alleviate his loneliness. At first, he didn't want to talk about Mom. Instead, he'd discuss the weather, sports, or island happenings. During the next phase he'd get angry and curse cigarettes. He'd curse the doctor who ordered the X-rays while Mom was pregnant with Jimmy. He'd blame anything and anyone for Mom's death. One day, I pulled off the highway to call Dad because I sensed his depression worsening.

"Dad," I said, "Are you really okay?"

"Yeah, I'm okay," he said with a strong voice.

"I want to make sure you're okay alone. You don't have any ideas to hurt yourself, do you, Daddy?"

"No-o-o," he said firmly. "Wait a minute. Let me put this cyanide pill down." He laughed and my chest collapsed with relief.

In the following seven years, I made multiple, extended visits to help out and keep him company. I'd stuff his freezer with single-serving portions of beef stew and soup. I'd do his laundry, iron his shirts, take him to doctor's appointments, and handle fix-it jobs around the house. Mostly, I'd keep him company. He'd watch Fox News while I worked on a crossword puzzle. In our tender time together, he didn't know his presence soothed me, diminishing any grief or guilt. It would take almost two years before Dad spoke about Mom with loving memories.

On the first Mother's Day without Mom, my sisters and I decided to visit Dad at his island home. It felt like the right place to be. Coincidentally, the local library was hosting an open house and they planned to recognize Mom's memory with a plaque. The donations sent in her name enabled them to purchase a new circulation desk. Dad asked me to say a few words about Mom at the gathering. I described my mother and her love of the island and love of reading.

"She never went to college but she self-educated her entire life."

When we got back to Dad's house, Jimmy called sounding

frantic.

"I can't find my beach towel!" he shouted. "Is it there?" Jimmy had the uncanny knack of knowing when something was going on without him. I felt awful about the exclusion but Dad said he simply couldn't cope with Jimmy's neediness at that time. I'd planned to visit Jimmy on my way home since my route took me right by his exit. "Good. You go see him," said Dad.

Jimmy persisted and wouldn't get off the phone.

"Jimmy, I'll look. I'm sure it's here somewhere," I said.

"Mom would have known where it is," he said angrily. I'd figure out later that, like many others who grieve, anger preceded Jimmy's sadness.

The year following Mom's death, Jimmy grew more anxious than usual before each holiday. He'd shop for answers and opportunities by asking each sister what the plans were. He wanted to make sure he wasn't being excluded. We all lived hundreds of miles apart from one another and none of us were in the mood to celebrate anything. I felt bad he was mourning alone yet couldn't be sure of his reactions to the loss. Whenever I spoke to him on the phone and asked how he felt about Mom, he either changed the subject or said nothing.

"Jimmy," I said, sitting across from him in a booth at a local restaurant, "Do you miss Mom?"

"Not really."

I didn't know what to make of it. Could he simply not express himself? Or could it have been he really didn't miss Mom because she had limited her visits with him the prior year? Her death came as a surprise to Jimmy. He wasn't aware of the risks of her surgery. Maybe he didn't miss her nagging. I didn't press him, figuring he needed to come to grips with the loss on his own terms. He'd talk when he felt ready.

"See that waitress over there," he said pointing. "I like her."

This was classic Jimmy. You might be talking about something important but he had his own agenda. I'd been trying to engage with him as brother and sister but his unrelated comment reoriented me to the fact that my role was still caregiver first.

30

Jimmy's grief took the form of medical issues. He became depressed and agitated with his roommates and the supervising staff at his residential complex. With every phone call he complained: It's too hot to work, they're bothering me, my stomach hurts, my ear hurts, I have hemorrhoids, I don't like it here, I want to live with Dad, I don't want to work anymore, I don't like the food, and on and on.

I dreaded seeing the caller ID. When that happened, I'd feel resentful to have to disrupt my family time at the dinner table and shore myself up for another heavy conversation. He had a couple of incidents at work. He drank liters of soda and his blood sugar level rocketed to 480 requiring an ambulance to come for him. He said he had chest pains. Another trip to the emergency room. His manager at the grocery store showed compassion each time by giving Jimmy gentle warnings and second chances. Jimmy should have been fired for literally sitting down on the job in the humidity of summer and bitter cold of winter. Finally, the manager agreed to put Jimmy on a leave of absence and transition him into retirement. This proved to be a workable solution for everyone. Jimmy considered himself ready to retire during an oppressively hot summer from a job he'd been complaining about anyway. I felt relieved and grateful to the manager for treating my brother with grace.

Although Jimmy had repeatedly said he was eager to retire, after it happened, he actually missed work. Specifically, he missed the paycheck. I think he missed money more than he missed our mother.

"I don't have any money," he'd frequently say. "Can you send me some money?" Sometimes I'd send him a check or gift certificate to a favorite store. Other times I'd fold a twenty-dollar bill in aluminum foil and insert it in a magazine or another small gift like socks or washcloths, both of which he could never seem to get enough of.

I cut back on my independent consulting work in order to devote time to managing Jimmy's issues. I was on edge receiving too many calls from the social workers (and wondering how many days would pass until another call came) reporting the same issues: Jimmy's not cooperating, he leaves the building without telling us, we're worried about his personal safety, he's not attentive when crossing the street, his eating is out of control, his sugar level is sky high.

Jimmy's coping skills usually meant he simply walked away from a situation. However, the specific talk about jumping off the balcony had set off an alarm like no other.

The resulting stay in the hospital felt like an eternity to me and probably to Jimmy, too, although in reality it was only a week. The nurse who managed the specialized unit for developmentally disabled adults told me Jimmy transitioned well. The behaviorist described Jimmy as likable, sociable, polite, insightful, and nurturing. She said he felt hopeless and his diabetes played a huge factor in his well-being. The constant theme of control, especially with food, affected his moods. She commented that Jimmy was a shy guy, and at the end of a group session he said, "I lost my mother four years ago." She gave him time to talk and validated his feelings. I don't know why Jimmy never directly expressed his grief to my sisters or me when we asked him how he felt. Perhaps he mimicked my father who kept his feelings to himself. Or maybe it was easier to express himself to strangers.

The hospital physician prescribed Wellbutrin. After four other anti-depressants, that's the one that worked.

When Jimmy returned home to his apartment eight days later, one kind social worker said, "He came back a new man." Jimmy had talked the whole way home. And he had a new feeling toward his apartment. After thirteen years, he finally called it home.

"Where's Albania?" he asked me, unrolling a map of the world when I visited him soon after. He'd always had a fascination with maps and I share his interest in geography.

"Albania. Why are you interested in that?" I asked.

"A guy I met in the hospital was from Albania." He searched with his pointer finger that guided him through all his reading and finally said, "Wow! That's far."

Jimmy's world had been rocked in more ways than one. The psychiatric hospital scared the living daylights out of him. He said he never wanted to go back there again. Aside from being stripped of all his belongings, sleeping on a hard bed bolted to the floor, and going to multiple therapy sessions, he met other troubled souls there. Many came from other parts of the world and had little to no family, much less the comfort of a home.

My world had been rocked, too. I knew this was the beginning of another stressful chapter in my life with Jimmy and I resented the disruption. I felt like I had a 200-pound sack on my shoulders. I resented Mom for leaving me with responsibility for Jimmy again. At the same time, I empathized for her—the loss, stress, and lack of freedom she endured. How much emotional energy would this exact from me? How would this affect my husband and daughters? Would I forsake them? I had sleepless nights and resorted to watching *House Hunters International* in the wee hours of the morning. Gray hair sprouted. I lost my appetite. I didn't smile often and frown lines emerged on my forehead. My daughters repeated themselves because my mind wandered from Jimmy to Daddy and the seemingly endless list of things I had to do to support them.

It would've been easy to stay in my pajamas, skip make-up and watch HGTV all day. I knew I couldn't do that. My family needed me. I vowed to continue daily calls to Dad to support him in his grief and loneliness. I didn't want to fall into a depression and need meds myself. I thought about what my doctor said to me after I'd left the business world and felt lost. She told me to create natural endorphins for my mental health. I resolved to keep up with morning walks and yoga practice. And always in the back of my mind a voice echoed to be strong, to get stuff done, to anticipate and fulfill the needs of my family.

My sisters and I agreed not to put any more pressure on Dad by telling him about Jimmy's episode. My father was staying at Alison's house. He had enough stress worrying if Hurricane Sandy demolished his house.

31

Less than a week after Jimmy settled back into his apartment, I met Alison at a rest stop on the Garden State Parkway in New Jersey. I was there to pick up Dad and bring him to my house. He'd been staying at Alison's since she'd brought him there before the hurricane hit. He needed a change of scenery. Since I worked part-time from home, he'd have me for company during the day.

"I hope my house is still standing," he'd say several times a day while gazing out my living room window at the falling leaves.

"We'll get you back home, Dad." I regularly checked Facebook posts about Long Beach Island and tried to get video of his street. Still, I couldn't determine what damage his house may have incurred. I reminded him that his house was built on one of the highest sections of the eighteen-mile-long barrier island. While I put on a brave face for him, I secretly worried about the possibility that he may have to remain at my house indefinitely and the impact it would have on my family and me.

We stayed glued to the television watching reports of the devastation in New Jersey and New York. Entire villages were obliterated. Thousands of people were suddenly homeless from what the meteorologists dubbed not just a hurricane, but

Superstorm Sandy. Roads were blocked and local shops were destroyed. Trees crushed cars and roofs. Electricity was out and power lines piled like spaghetti on the streets. The subway was submerged in water and bacteria. People searched for food and shelter. Hotels were filled, some without generators. Schools and businesses remained closed while the governors of New Jersey and New York traipsed from one ruined town to another reassuring citizens they'd rebuild.

Three days later we learned from another islander that Dad's house was still standing with no visible damage. However, we couldn't be sure what we'd find once we got inside. Another week passed before Dad and I drove the six hours back to New Jersey on a sunny, cold day in November. On the drive, he regaled me with stories of his Army service. He'd served in the Philippines building bridges and wound up in the hospital for a week after contracting malaria.

"Did you see any action, Dad?"

"No. And I thank Truman for that. He dropped the bomb when I was on a ship to Okinawa. The President saved my life."

As we turned off the Garden State Parkway and drove closer to Dad's town, we saw damaged boats that had floated from the bay onto the streets. Sand, dirt, and debris carpeted the highway medians and shoulders of the road. Docks and marina pilings were strewn like mounds of Lincoln Logs. By the time we turned onto his deserted street, we breathed a sigh of relief to see all the houses still standing.

The gas line to the house had been inspected and tagged. That permitted Dad to move back into his little nest. He was so happy to be back sitting at the dining room table opening the stack of mail that had accumulated. Shortly afterward, he napped while I ran errands. While doing so, I found a contractor working on another house and pleaded with him to come over to Dad's house to examine the crawlspace where the insulation and ductwork were located. Contractors were booked solid. Residents had to wait or pay a premium for services. Carpenters, HazMat experts, plumbers, and other tradespeople had traveled from out of state to help with restoring the island. Trucks with license plates from as far as California parked at convenience stores where their weary owners loaded up on coffee, sandwiches, and supplies.

Less than a minute later, the contractor crawled out from under the house, dusted his pants and hands, and gave me a foreboding look.

"Get your father out of here immediately," he said while we stood on the back patio.

"What? Why?"

"See this," he said pointing to a gray line on the beige aluminum siding. "This is how high the water rose. About two feet above street level. The insulation in the crawlspace is soaked and starting to mold."

My jaw dropped. Just when I thought we were out of the woods, another setback for Dad. Selfishly, I thought: *more work, more work for me*. I had to stay strong for him, not knowing what this repair would cost in time and money, not to mention the emotional toll and inconvenience on Dad. The only reason I was able to keep my perspective was because I knew that thousands of other innocent people lost their homes, businesses, and more. At least Dad had flood insurance.

On the one hand, I'd be glad for Dad's company on the return trip home. On the other hand, I dreaded another long, anxiety-filled drive for both of us. And then what? How long would he stay? Would he wind up living with me permanently?

That thought scared me because my family life would be turned upside down to accommodate him. What about his prescriptions and doctor appointments? How would I solve all this? I turned and saw Dad holding the screen door ajar.

"Everything okay?" he asked with a hopeful smile.

"Dad, come here," I said taking his hand. "Look at this," I said, pointing to the water line. "All the insulation is soaked. We have to get this fixed, replace all the ducts. It's not safe to stay here. We have to pack up right now and move."

His smile disappeared and the color drained from his face.

"I thought everything was okay."

"So did I, Dad." I wanted to cry for him but stuck to the facts. There was no time to commiserate.

"It's not safe, Mr. Poggi," said the contractor.

One of my mother's phrases echoed in my mind: *The more you do, the more you can do.* She'd say this optimistically when housecleaning, after finishing a great tennis match, or anytime she felt energized. She wanted to demonstrate that if you just kept busy doing, then there was no time to doubt yourself, be fearful, or be paralyzed with indecision. As a deep thinker, Mom knew the importance of staying physically active, even with housework, to keep negative feelings at bay. I'd learn this, too, especially when Dad or Jimmy's needs required my intervention. However, I would not imitate my mother by running hard and fast in a crisis and then crashing on the couch for a week from exhaustion and mental fatigue.

Within ten minutes, I packed our suitcases, bagged some food, turned off the lights, and locked the house. I moved Dad a mile down the road to my cousin's beach cottage that was unaffected by the storm. I resettled him and stayed the night. The next morning I reluctantly headed back to Massachusetts alone. While the drive forced me to concentrate on the route and traffic, my head spun with guilt and fear about leaving him alone, even though he had insisted I go home to my family. I worried he'd fall down the stairs of the raised ranch. I was certain he wouldn't eat properly, wouldn't ask for help, and would get depressed. A week later, an angel named Marianne made an offer for Dad to stay at her summer home directly next door. It had electric heat and a bedroom and full bath on the first floor. He stayed for a month watching laborers come and go as they repaired his house.

All the local contractors were booked but I'd found another contractor who would become our second angel. A lifesaver named Gabe had driven all the way from San Diego and picked up a colleague in southern Illinois to easily secure work on the ravaged island. They suited up in HazMat gear and completed the nasty job of removing the filthy ducts and other debris from under the house. They packed all the contents of Dad's house and carried lots of boxes into the garage. They tore up all the soiled carpeting only to find asbestos tile under a portion of it. That led to another contractor who specialized in asbestos removal, days of large-scale fans blowing the house clean and clear, and a third contractor for state-mandated testing and re-testing of air quality.

Each day I'd call Dad to find out what was happening at the house. One delay caused another. One project repair precipitated another. Dad was frustrated. The email thread between tradespeople and me got long quickly. The house needed interior paint, new baseboards, new carpeting, carpentry, and more. I tracked all the calls and documents for the repair of Dad's house. The copious calls to contractors and municipal representatives exhausted me. My adrenaline surged by day and by night I was restless and had trouble sleeping, thinking of the next day's to-do list.

Lynne handled all the insurance matters and dealt with FEMA red tape. Alison zipped down to visit Dad whenever she could. She lived the closest at a two-hour drive. She'd audit his checkbook, bring him meals, and keep him company. She even managed a quiet birthday celebration for him. My eighty-five-year-old father had never slept around so much–six beds in seven weeks.

Lynne, Alison, Jimmy, my husband, and I finally moved Dad back into his house two weeks before Christmas. It felt comforting to be with my sisters and Jimmy. We laughed as Alison delivered her classic zingers and Lynne moved at her signature lightning speed. Mom would have been proud to see us wiping everything down, so reminiscent of her famous spring cleaning. Jimmy was a huge help, willingly doing whatever we asked: unwrapping dishes, moving the big hutch, carrying trash to the curb, sweeping up. We were all relieved and happy to get Dad back into the comfort of his own home and his routine.

"Where's my lamp?" he asked from his lounge chair as we traipsed in and out with boxes and furniture. "How about my favorite clock? I've had that clock a long time, you know."

"We'll get everything back exactly the way you had it, Dad," I assured him.

He supervised from his chair as we earnestly recreated the interior of his home. It took ten hours. Despite our exhaustion, Lynne had cooked a roast beef dinner at Marianne's house next door. With great relief, we gathered around the table and celebrated an early Christmas like never before.

"I'm going for a walk," said my husband. "You five need to be together now." It was the first time the Poggi family of six sat as a family of five. A bittersweet pall hung over the table.

Two weeks later, on New Year's Eve day, Dad called.

"Joyce?" I heard his voice straining. He'd called me from his cell phone, which, thankfully, he'd taken with him before rushing out of the house.

"What is it, Daddy?" I asked urgently, scared to hear his response.

"I fell. I can't get up."

"Stay on the line, Daddy. I'm calling 911 from my other phone." It took a couple of frantic attempts and transfers from my Massachusetts location to get in touch with New Jersey emergency medics. While we waited, I asked Dad exactly where he was in the house.

"I'm in the driveway. Near the garage," he said, his voice fading.

"The driveway?" I asked, shocked. The temperatures had hovered near freezing. I later discovered he'd lain there for two hours, weak and nearly voiceless, trying to get help. Very few people stay on the island in winter and even fewer year-round residents drive down his street. The thought of him lying there helpless on the gravel driveway at the back of the house distressed me. I later learned he'd called 911 but never pressed the "Send" button. Fortunately, he remembered my number and was able to dial it in the frigid cold, after a few attempts.

Once again there was no time to think, only do. First I called for an ambulance and then I called my sisters. Alison got to Dad at the hospital within two hours. She stayed a couple of days until I arrived. I stayed for a week until Lynne took her turn.

"Lynne," I said. "We have to check out assisted living facilities." I had collected several brochures from the hospital social worker.

"He's not ready," she insisted.

"He might be. We have to plan now. Let's at least get him on the waiting list," I said. In the midst of this new crisis, I toured a nearby facility. The image of Dad lying in the driveway alone in the numbing cold of the last day of a tumultuous year crushed me. My greatest fear was him falling again or having a stroke or heart attack alone in the house with no neighbors to help him. I hated the thought of him in pain. It made my heart ache. I tried to contain my worry with deep breathing.

Before bringing Dad back to his home, I hired a contractor to install grab bars from his kitchen door to the walkway out back. Once settled, I called the local Catholic parish and learned about a senior nutrition program. Finally, the church had come through with a benefit for my family.

Soon after this mayhem, it was clear Dad could only handle so much. He'd been managing Jimmy's finances since Mom had died four years earlier. I interacted with the social workers, banks, and other legal entities to transfer bill paying to The Arc with oversight and audits done by Alison, who lived closest to Jimmy.

I had been fielding calls from The Arc for several years but now instructed the social workers to bypass my father entirely and instead call me directly for all matters pertaining to Jimmy. The emotional toll stressed Dad. He'd suffered with heart disease and I wanted to do anything to relieve him of stress. I selectively apprised Dad of Jimmy's issues only when I deemed he was ready to hear it.

Dad willingly relinquished the responsibility of Jimmy. The situation reminded me of Mom in her last summer when she voluntarily resigned her post as caregiver, administrator, and advocate (never as parent, though). Dad's resignation would be the harbinger of a returning role for me as primary advocate for Jimmy. It was a foregone conclusion that I would take the reins. Mentally preparing myself for the responsibility made the time of acceptance easier than if it had been thrust upon me suddenly.

A few months after Jimmy returned home from the psychiatric hospital, I got another call. Jimmy was agitated again and said he was going to die anyway. By this time, he was enrolled in a day program where he didn't quite fit in. The participants included special needs adults with lower cognitive abilities than Jimmy's as well as many senior citizens. (A few years later, I advocated for Jimmy's transfer to another more stimulating day program where he became happier and challenged.)

When I called him, he asked about my father's best friend Sam who was dying of cancer. Jimmy feared our father's death, too. And Jimmy always got anxious before his birthday or any holiday. It was a week before his birthday, and what turned out to be only days before Sam's death.

"Jimmy," I said, "I know you're sad about Sam, but there's nothing you or the doctors can do. Think of the nice times you had with Sam."

"Uh . . ." Big exhale and pause. "Okay," he said, his voice trailing.

"Jimmy, the staff told me you're saying you want to kill yourself. If you keep saying that, you'll end up in the hospital again and may never come home. Is that what you want?" This wasn't the compassionate thing to say but Jimmy needed to be shaken and I knew when to do that.

"No." He'd calmed down.

"Jimmy, tell me, what's the matter?" I'd envision him standing in his room alone in the dark. He had a habit of keeping the lights turned low, when they were on at all.

"I don't know how to make friends, Joyce."

I thought of all the times he'd come barreling through the back door in his hockey gear after a game with the neighborhood boys. I remembered his belly laughs and animation while playing table hockey and Matchbox cars down the basement. He made friends easily as a kid but found it difficult as an adult. Beginning in his twenties, his friends were my parents' friends.

"The way to make friends, Jimmy, is to be a friend. Who would you like to be friends with?"

"Arthur."

"Okay. Go over and knock on Arthur's door. Ask him if he'd like to play cards or do a jigsaw puzzle with you. Do you think you can do that?"

Sigh. "Okay. Yeah," he said, the tone of his voice lifting, "I can do that."

"Sure you can. You're a great guy, Jimmy. And smile. It helps you feel better."

After every call with Jimmy, I exhaled a sigh of relief. I'd talk him through whatever hurdle he faced, hang up, and then wonder how long it would be until his next call with a problem to be solved. I recorded every incident in a binder and then reported the same to Lynne and Alison.

I stopped reporting details about Jimmy to my husband, at first because doing so got me riled up again. Repeating the same issues helped neither of us and afterward I'd feel tired and sad. By refraining, the result was that I felt lighter. I wanted to hold on to that feeling of lightness so I made sure to exercise every morning either with a yoga class or a long walk. Finally, during one of those reflective walks I told myself to let go of the incessant worry and anticipated anxiety. I couldn't live in a state of sadness my whole life because of Jimmy's special needs. I saw what it did to my mother and vowed not to let myself fall into a cycle of regret. Moreover, I didn't want my daughters to witness in me the depression that I witnessed in my mother.

32

My parents had made a brave and wise decision moving Jimmy into a supervised apartment. In retrospect, they said moving him in his early twenties instead of his early forties might have helped him to assimilate better. Nonetheless, they did what they thought was right at the time. Only when I became a parent could I understand their logic.

I'm grateful to and admire my mother for seeking out this living arrangement for Jimmy. She was adamant not to disrupt the family life of Lynne, Alison, and me by having Jimmy live with any of us. She insisted Jimmy remain in his supervised apartment. She wanted him to be semi-independent and refused to consider him living anywhere else. It is the most heroic, unsung gift she gave to her daughters.

The staff managing the program and apartments where Jimmy lives have challenging jobs. I admire them for the work they do. They interact with residents with varied developmental disabilities, coordinate copious doctors appointments, provide transportation, handle financial and legal matters, keep detailed documentation on each resident, make astute observations and recommendations, coordinate day programs and social outings, take them shopping, resolve conflict, communicate with various constituents–family members, physicians, supervisors, state and federal workers—and manage plenty of behind-the-scenes details I can't imagine. Most importantly, they care for the health and safety of Jimmy. It's a thankless, under-recognized job that takes immeasurable patience and compassion. For all these reasons and more, my family and I are grateful to all the people at The Arc.

Lynne, Alison, and I participate as much as we can in Jimmy's life—sometimes one more than the others, depending on what's happening in our own families and jobs. I continue to take on the role as primary communicator and documenter. After all, I've been primed for it my whole life. I feel reassured knowing I have the support of my sisters and we always consult with each other on decisions impacting Jimmy's life. We are lock step in our fervent desire to help him any way we can. It's difficult since none of us live near each other or Jimmy, so we have to coordinate multi-hour drives. We rely on three-way phone calls.

I work hard to keep positive and timely communications with Jimmy's staff of social workers. That line of work sees a lot of turnover so I'm frequently being introduced to a new staff member. More importantly, it presents difficulty for Jimmy because he's constantly being addressed by a new face. It's hard for him to build trust and relationships with staff members who come and go. However, a few workers have been caring for Jimmy for several years and the consistency makes relations easier. I was flattered when one supervisor said to me, "You're like the poster family," regarding the love and support we provide to Jimmy and the level of interaction we have with the staff.

I know this is my role and will be for as long as I live. It's something I finally came to accept soon after Mom died. When

I was in my twenties and on my own, I finally felt free of the responsibilities of Jimmy and thought they were all behind me. Then when I had children of my own and the hours of the day were consumed with my own motherhood and a full-time job, I didn't give much thought to Jimmy's trials. Even when Jimmy moved to supervised living, I figured it was someone else's job to worry about him. I was wrong. The worry never ends. Although he lives semi-independently and has professional social workers to help him, he still needs his advocate in me. And he still needs the sister in me.

Jimmy has good days and better days. The meds help. He'll be attending plenty of doctor appointments for years to come, like many senior citizens.

What also helps is the active day program run by the Easter Seals that Jimmy attends. It took a year of my advocacy to get him enrolled so he can now enjoy day trips to local venues with friends of similar capabilities.

"Everybody's got something," Dad often said to me. In his later years, we'd talk about who fought cancer, who had a troubled grandchild, who was dealing with dementia, lost their eyesight, or needed a wheelchair.

I know I'll be receiving calls from Jimmy's social workers until one of us dies. I've accepted there will always be the extra weight in my life. I used to try to shed that weight, but learned to embrace it. I view it as my foundation. Being Jimmy's sister forces me to be brave in the face of adversity, to show compassion where I might otherwise want to walk away, to do things that appear hard to do. It's a gift that humbles me.

$\sim$

"Joyce, you should have seen my golf game today!" he says. "I putted about twenty feet on the ninth hole!"

Jimmy took up golf in his late fifties. He loves it and I'm relieved and delighted he finally found a hobby to keep him motivated. He subscribes to three golf magazines and posts articles about techniques on his walls. Jimmy taught himself how to use a computer tablet and spends hours on word and number games. He loves to go online to research a geographical point of interest or any kind of statistic such as his favorite golfer's age. He keeps abreast of major league sports by reading several newspapers every day and will give me a 6:45 wake-up call to report the latest baseball trade.

Jimmy's vocabulary has grown from all his reading. He initiates conversation about current events. He laughs more and stays on the phone longer. He asks questions about brain injuries to football players, says it's time for our soldiers to come home, and wants to know how he can be sure that our mother is watching over him from heaven.

"Jimmy," I say, "how about I bring my clubs next week when I visit? We can go golfing together."

"Yeah?" he says with a lift in his voice.

"Sure. I'm not very good but it'll be fun. Just you and me."

"Okay." I can hear his excitement and it softens my heart.

The following week we approach the golf course on a glorious afternoon. A few clouds dot the summer sky and the tall evergreens sway on either side of us. Jimmy tees off at the first hole and blasts the ball straight down the fairway. He stares into the green expanse, estimating his distance. I notice a slight curl up one side of his mouth as he bends to retrieve the tee.

"Wow, Jimmy, you have a powerful swing," I say reaching for my driver.

"Thank you," he says evenly, sliding the club into his bag.

Swoosh! My ball flies a mere seventy yards and hooks left.

"Try to hit 'em straight, Joyce," he says strutting ahead of me, eager for his next shot.

I smile and bow my head. Finally, my brother takes the lead.

Eagle Ridge Golf Course
Lakewood, New Jersey
April 2017

Acknowledgments

I didn't plan to write a memoir. A year after my mother died, I took a one-day creative writing class, and an essay poured out of me. It was the patterning scene. The rest of the story morphed over several years, with occasional breaks. I kept asking myself why I was writing this until it finally dawned on me. I wrote it for my daughters, Kristin and Melissa.

Thank you . . .
Kathleen Molloy Nollet, my loyal writing partner and friend. You pushed me forward every time I wanted to retreat.

Thank you . . .
Christopher J. Boginski, Kelly Pelissier, and Betsy Johns.

Thank you . . .
Mary Cullin, Bridget Rawding, Martha Schaefer, Grub Street, and early readers.

Thank you . . .
Kristin Olson, and the community of Home Yoga. Many *aha* moments came to me on and off the mat.

Thank you . . .
Claire Cedrone, Anna DiCanzio, and Dolores Kornblatt—my mother's dearest friends who filled in the blanks of my early childhood.

Thank you . . .
Lynne and Alison, for your support, loyalty, and sense of humor.

Thank you . . .
Mom, for believing in me, and for modeling the love of reading and writing.

Thank you . . .
Dad, for your devotion and encouragement, and for telling me to sell the piano and replace it with a writing desk.

Thank you . . .
Gary, for your love, patience, and support.

And always, with love and pride,
Thank you, Jimmy. You inspire and motivate me every day.

85925529R00152

Made in the USA
Columbia, SC
02 January 2018